Sustaining the Common Good

Sustaining the Common Good

A Christian Perspective on the Global Economy

John B. Cobb, Jr.

The Pilgrim Press
Cleveland, Ohio

The Pilgrim Press, Cleveland, Ohio 44115
© 1994 by John B. Cobb, Jr.

All rights reserved. Published 1994

Printed in the United States of America
on acid-free paper

99 98 97 96 95 94   5 4 3 2 1

Library of Congress Cataloging-in-Publication Data

Cobb, John B.
Sustaining the common good : a Christian perspective on the global
economy / John B. Cobb, Jr.
p.   cm.
Includes bibliographical references and index.
ISBN 0-8298-1010-2
1. International economic relations—Moral and ethical aspects.
2. Economic development—Religious aspects—Christianity.
3. Sustainable development—International cooperation.   I. Title.
HF1359.C63   1994
337—dc20   94-23379
CIP

Contents

Preface

In the summer of 1969, my son Cliff helped open my eyes
to what human beings are doing to our shared natural environment. For the first time I saw the meaning of the finitude of the world and began to understand the pressure of
human activity upon its capacities. I saw that the problem
of pollution did not go away when the winds blew the car-
bon monoxide away from Los Angeles out to sea. I saw, instead, that the capacity of nature to handle our wastes was
declining as the quantity of these wastes grew larger. Species were dying out, and natural resources were being exhausted. While the carrying capacity of the planet declined,
human population continued to grow and per capita consumption in rich countries continued to rise. I realized that
simply increasing the total economic activity of the planet
would not solve the problems of the world's poor. In short,
I saw that the ways I had previously envisaged that human
problems were to be progressively alleviated would not
work, that they only hastened catastrophe.

During the 1970s I was preoccupied with the realization
that human beings were on a collision course with ecologi-

cal disaster. As a theologian I gave much of my attention to the changes that are needed in Christian teaching and in Western thought in general if we are to turn in another direction. I was pleased that the churches began to take part in this project and that ecological concerns became part of the wider culture. But I was troubled that even as beliefs and attitudes improved, the objective situation grew worse.

I came to the conclusion that the course of events on the planet is primarily determined by the economy. I saw that the economy is little affected by these improvements in thought, and that until economic thinking was changed, other changes would have minimal effect. I became convinced that practical economic thinking follows the lines laid down by standard economic theory and that this must be challenged.

In consequence, I occupied myself during much of the eighties with the issues of economic theory. Why was this theory so impervious to the changes in thought about the environment taking placing in the surrounding culture? What were its assumptions? What could one learn from them, and how could one criticize them? Could economic theory be changed so as to become a better guide to economic practice in a world of limits?

I asked the economist Herman Daly to work with me on a book on economic theory. In 1989 we published *For the Common Good*.[1] I felt that I now had a fairly adequate perspective on what is wrong with orthodox economic theory from the point of view of a Christian who affirms the preferential option for the poor and the integrity of creation. From the point of view of the positive conclusions of that book, the dominant course of economic practice in the world today moves in the wrong direction.

During the late eighties and early nineties I have been trying to spell out what is wrong with the policies to which world leaders are committed as well as the reversal of direction that is needed. Mostly this has been in individual speeches and a number of published essays.

When Pilgrim Press asked me if I would write a book on economics for the church, it occurred to me that some of these speeches and essays might be the foundation for such a book. I looked them over and selected some for this purpose. This book is the result. It includes two chapters that were written originally for publication. One of these, "Against Free Trade," was published in *Theology and Public Policy*,[2] and I am grateful for permission to use it again here. The other, "Christian Faith and the Degradation of Creation," was written for a project that remains incomplete.

The arguments contained in these chapters are not fully developed. They presuppose the theory worked out in *For the Common Good*. Nevertheless, I hope that they explain my reasons for believing that the present course of the global economy is disastrous. I hope also that the general shape of the alternative will become clear to the reader.

No essay was written with any of the others in mind, and I was thinking many of the same thoughts as I wrote each one; thus, some topics were treated in more than one. I have reduced, but not eliminated, such repetitions. The essays cannot but contain similar arguments as they are all written from the same point of view. I hope that the parallel arguments in successive chapters, for example, those against the widespread commitment to economic growth, will have cumulative force for the reader, rather than merely eliciting boredom. At any rate, I am satisfied that the main points made in each chapter and the great majority of the contents are mutually supplementary rather than repetitive. As a whole they represent a Christian criticism of major political and economic developments occurring in our world and offer proposals for their reversal. The proposals follow from the theory developed with Daly, and there are repeated references back to our book, but they draw forth its implications around more specific topics.

Discussions of current issues are likely to become dated
quickly, and I have revised lightly throughout to deal with
this problem. For example, as I write, the House of Representatives has just voted in favor of the North American
Free Trade Agreement (NAFTA), whereas all the chapters
were originally written when its fate was uncertain. Even
so, the broader issues illustrated by this treaty will continue to be urgent ones for a long time. Since the discussion
of NAFTA is for the sake of illumining these broader issues, I have made only minor changes to reflect the current
situation, believing that my discussion as a whole remains
relevant. Also, I learned too late to change the text in chapter 4 that in 1993 the World Bank withdrew support from
the Narmada Valley Project.[3]

Since I did not have publication in mind when preparing
most of this material, I did not keep a careful record of my
sources. Tracking them down has not been easy. I want to
express particular appreciation to Dr. Robert Benson of
Loyola Law School for his assistance.

Throughout the book I frequently speak of the Third
World. With the end of the sharp division of the First and
Second Worlds, this is no longer appropriate, so I have ex-
perimented with alternate terms. For internal consistency,
however, I have returned to the familiar, if anachronistic,
term Third World.

The first chapter is the most general. It presents theological reasons for adopting the stance from which the other
chapters are written. It also introduces some elements of
economic theory that are assumed and developed in later
chapters. The second chapter, a lecture given at a conference funded by the Wisconsin Council for the Humanities,
offers my theological critique of economics and of what I
call economism in a broader humanistic and historical context. The third chapter was written for a conference on
"ecocommunities." My objection to the individualism of
economics and its destruction of community is mentioned

in the earlier chapters; here the positive importance of community as the unit of economic development is the major theme.

The remaining three chapters deal with topics that are widely discussed among those interested in public policy. They bring the perspective developed in *For the Common Good* and in the earlier chapters to bear on these topics. These are the debt crisis, viewed here chiefly from the point of view of the poor in the debtor nations; the issue of free trade, with NAFTA as the main illustration; and the new world order affirmed, but little described, by George Bush. The topics are closely connected, but separate treatment seems to be warranted.

Any author is likely to exaggerate the importance of her or his work. Although I have no illusions about the quality of the book as an integrated whole, I do believe that no issue can be more critical for humanity in general, and for the Christian community in particular, than the one it treats: the acceptability of the economic policies that shape our lives and destiny. I know that there are conscientious Christians who understand these policies and still affirm them. That is a mystery to me. There are others who know they are wrong but believe that nothing can be done to change them. That is even more distressing.

Indeed, the present course is already proving a disaster for hundreds of millions of people. UNICEF estimates that "for almost nine hundred million people, approximately one-sixth of mankind, the march of human progress has now become a retreat." The major cause is the debt crisis discussed in chapter 4 and the structural adjustments required of debtor countries by the International Monetary Fund. "In the thirty-seven poorest nations, spending per head on health has been reduced by 50 percent. . . . It is children who are bearing the heaviest burden. . . . At least half a million young children have died in the last twelve months as a result."[4]

In "The Coming Anarchy," Robert Kaplan's description of the collapse of the natural environment and social order in much of West Africa shows how far the disaster has gone there. The forest cover is gone, replaced by swamps and wasteland. Sewers provide the only water available for millions. Untreatable malaria has taken over and deters outsiders from even visiting. AIDS gains ground rapidly. It is hard to envision a hopeful scenario. Kaplan points out that some of the factors that have led to this catastrophe are at work in many other parts of the world.[5]

The present course of the global economy will draw us all into catastrophe. Christians must not continue to ignore these matters, leaving them to the "experts." The expertise of the experts, even those who are personally Christian, is shaped by assumptions that Christians cannot accept, as I will demonstrate. To continue, in spite of this, to sanction policies that are already causing untold suffering is simply not acceptable. I hope that this book can contribute to awakening the people of God to what is happening and to the Christian alternatives that the situation still allows.

1
Christian Faith and the Degradation of Creation

Degradation of the earth began occurring even before the advent of the human species. Meteors, volcanic eruptions, ice ages, and other disasters throughout planetary history have set back the development of the biosphere locally and sometimes even globally, sometimes wiping out thousands of species. Nevertheless, prior to the emergence of human beings, the biosphere grew richer and richer.

From quite early times human beings contributed to the degradation of their environment. Hunting and gathering peoples hunted some species to extinction, and sometimes their use of fire degraded the landscape. Still, on the whole, hunting and gathering peoples functioned less as degraders of the biosphere and more as part of it, adding to its richness.

Systematic degradation of creation began with the domestication of animals and plants. Animals now are bred for traits convenient and useful to human beings, but counter to intelligence and adaptability. Furthermore, domesticated animals graze in ways that degrade the landscape, whereas their wild counterparts do not. Some of the world's great deserts are testimony to their ability, under human management, to destroy the biosphere.

The domestication of plants also has led to the loss of once-fertile areas to desert. Erosion results from the breaking up of the soil for planting, and salinization from the irrigation widely practiced from very ancient times. In tropical areas, the soil often turns to rock when the trees are cleared to make room for agriculture. The planet is dotted with evidence of these activities.

The growth of human population that accompanies civilization has almost always accelerated degradation. In addition to the intensified pressure on the land inherent in both pastoral and agricultural lifestyles, the demands on forests are heavy. Deforestation leaves hillsides vulnerable to erosion, which not only degrades the hills but also muddies once-clean rivers and causes floods downstream. While various systems of belief have helped to protect the environment against human ravages, none have been very effective over long periods of time once cities are built and the population has grown. Taoism, for example, could not protect the Chinese mountains from deforestation, despite its sensitivity to nature.

The modern degradation of the earth, in some respects, may be considered simply a continuation of this long human history. The rapid growth of human population has its inevitable consequences regardless of the accompanying beliefs. Nevertheless, there are qualitative differences between the degradation of the planet in recent times and that which preceded it.

Previously, human effects on the earth were local; now they are planetary. Previously, most of them were gradual and largely unplanned; now the changes are rapid, and many are under conscious human control. Previously, the long-term consequences of human actions were poorly understood; now we continue the process of degrading the earth with our eyes open. Previously, the system of belief on which civilizations operated had only sporadic and secondary effect on the extent of their despoliation of their environment; now we confront decisions that clearly involve fundamental commitments.

We are free as a species to continue to accelerate the degradation of the earth or to slow and finally reverse this process. Our decision depends on the deepest convictions and fundamental commitments that constitute the religious level of our being. For many people this level is not expressed in their official involvement in a traditional religious community. Especially in the West since the Enlightenment, explicitly religious traditions have been assigned more limited roles, with the basic belief structure being determined elsewhere.

In the past few decades, the religious fervor with respect to environmental concerns has been largely disconnected from traditional religious institutions. Many of the most deeply religious people have felt the need for a new vision attuned to the realities of the world and free from the destructive baggage of the great traditions. They hoped this new religious community would arise from the debris of the great traditions, rallying the energies of all humanity for the salvation of the earth.

However, hope for such a new religion has faded, and even those most estranged from the religious traditions have become more interested in their potential for support of the healing of the earth. Some of us have believed all along that the current situation calls for the repentance and renewal of these traditions, and specifically of Christianity, rather than the effort to produce a religion disconnected from the great traditions. Although it is already very late, there are increasing signs that repentance and renewal are occurring, and that the major traditions will shift from being enemies of the earth to being its friends.

Before we ask directly what the stance of Christianity should be, it is important to examine the dominant ideology out of which the most determinative decisions about the fate of the earth are now being made. Many Christians still support that ideology, and critical evaluation of it will give a healthy dose of realism to theological reflection. The ideology in question is that of the European Enlightenment, which found its purest expression in the eighteenth century. In the history of thought it was severely criticized in the nineteenth century. Academic philosophy and theology today are far removed from the deism associated with the Enlightenment, as are contemporary painting and literature. Thus it may seem strange to identify that ideology as the currently determinative one, but the decisions that determine how we act in relation to the natural world are only sporadically and secondarily affected by these developments in intellectual history.

From the beginning, the economy has determined how human beings have dealt with their environment, and this is still true. But in modern times, the actual economy is deeply affected by economic theory, as expressed in eighteenth-century Enlightenment thinking. The connection between the Enlightenment and economic theory is no mystery. Every textbook on the history of economics points to the views of Scottish philosopher Adam Smith as the turning point in economic thought.[1] What happened before him is viewed as pre-scientific anticipation of the science of economics, and Smith initiated the line of thinking that has become contemporary economics. In spite of the great advances since his time, he established the basic assumptions, and no one can doubt that Smith was an Enlightenment thinker.

Much of what needs to be understood about economic theory follows from Smith's view of the human being. Smith knew that human beings can be deeply affected by sympathy for others. But he saw that this operated in quite narrow circles. In the economic order people provide us the goods and services we need, whether they feel sympathy for us or not, because it is in their interest to do so. If all act according to their best interest, it turns out, goods and services flow in the most favorable way.

Smith knew that the self-interested individual is an abstraction from the fullness of human beings, especially from the human capacity for sympathy. But he was convinced that this abstraction clarifies the way human beings function in economic relationships. Hence the abstractness of this model could be largely ignored for purposes of understanding the economic order. Smith himself, in fact, showed awareness of other dimensions of human beings, such as patriotism, as relevant to the functioning of the economy, but because he did not make these his theme, the science of economics ignored them. His individual actor in the market became *Homo economicus*.

Homo economicus as worker wants to procure as many goods and services as possible in exchange for as little work as possible. *Homo economicus* as owner of capital wants to invest in the way that will bring the largest possible returns. Obviously he will pay as little as possible to his workers. Much of the reflection of the early economists was on this situation and its effects on wages and profits.

The quest for maximum returns on investments has another effect, however. It leads to specialization. Instead of one skilled artisan making a product, such as a pin, from raw materials, a group of workers, each performing just one simple operation, produces pins on an assembly line. Total production is vastly increased. Specialization dramatically improves productivity, which is the total product divided by the number of hours of human labor.

One such pin factory can produce far more pins than are needed in the local community. Hence, rather than each community having its own pin factory, it is better for the neighboring community to specialize in something else, perhaps hats. A third community will specialize in shoes, and so forth. The result is that the same total number of hours of labor will produce far more goods, and hence the people of these communities collectively will be more prosperous. (Unfortunately, there is no assurance of equitable distribution of the new wealth.) The size of the market, that is, of the area in which goods and services can flow freely, determines how far specialization can go. The larger the market, the greater the specialization possible, and the greater the productivity. The greater the productivity, the greater the prosperity.

The economic system works best when left to itself. Competition leads investors to supply what is most wanted and keeps the prices as low as possible. Specialization is encouraged, also to keep prices low, and is accompanied by an increase in productivity and the supply of goods. Government interference can only hamper this positive working of the market. The economic ideal is laissez-faire within each country and the elimination of national boundaries as barriers to trade. Free trade in this sense is a central goal of most economists.

Through most of the two centuries in which economic theory has been developed, economic nationalism in fact remained strong. Hence free trade was constantly restricted by perceived national interests. In the late twentieth century, however, nationalism has subsided to a remarkable degree, and other economic considerations have become dominant. The Reagan and Bush administrations pushed free trade with impressive single-mindedness as the solution to economic problems everywhere. The Clinton administration shows no signs of disputing the basic theory, although it is more concerned with labor conditions and the environment. In the Uruguay round of negotiations on the General Agreement on Tariffs and Trade (GATT), the economists' dream is coming close to reality. If adopted, GATT will wipe out much government intervention in the markets within nations and also remaining restrictions on trade across national borders. Economically speaking, we will take another giant step toward becoming one world.

How should a Christian respond to this system of beliefs that shapes the activity of so many committed and idealistic people? Let us consider first what is attractive in it and then its limitations.

Adam Smith did not write as a Calvinist theologian, but his view of the human being is not far removed from that of many Scottish Calvinists of his day. They, too, were suspicious of expecting too much from human sympathy or love. They recognized with Smith that most people's actions were basically selfish. They differed, of course, in that they deplored this selfishness and sought forgiveness for it. But it was easy for them to accept that a realistic account of the economic order would describe it, not in terms of love, but in terms of self-interest. The brilliant success of economists in describing market activity in these terms is further confirmation of the fruitfulness of the model. The Christian can hardly dispute this.

Secondly, most Christians rejoice in the success of the economy in producing more goods and services and eventually bringing affluence to a high percentage of the people in the First World. We may admire poverty when it is chosen by the saint for the fulfillment of a particular vocation, but we regard imposed and inescapable poverty as a degradation to be fought. Hence, the increase of material wealth is a great good, and economic theory deserves credit for its contribution to the attainment of affluence.

Third, Christians, who for several centuries have feared nationalism as the greatest idolatry of the modern world, can only rejoice at the role played by economics in overcoming its limitations. Knowing that human beings constitute one great family under God, that God cares alike for all, Christians have sought to extend human concern across national boundaries. The erosion of these boundaries and of the nationalism associated with them is surely something to be celebrated.

Nevertheless, from a Christian point of view, the model is seriously flawed, and the effects of shaping the economy according to the model have been severely damaging. If the policies derived from this model are continued much longer they will be disastrous. Hence, the full application of the economic ideal that we are now witnessing forces us to think clearly about the Christian ideal.

The economic model describes how production increases with the increase of specialization and the growth of the size of the market. It does not take into account the input of raw materials in the production process or the emission of wastes into the environment. From a Christian point of view, it limits itself to human production and ignores the creation. This feature of the model has had damaging effects from the beginning, but they were on the whole local and sporadic. Now the scale of human production is so large that these damaging effects are global and catastrophic. The goal of increasing production still more, the only goal to which the dominant economic model is adapted, encourages the further, and intensified, degradation of creation.

The aim at unceasing growth and the understanding of *Homo economicus* are closely connected. While the doctrine of human sinfulness supports the view of *Homo economicus* as aiming only at individual advantage, this does not exhaust Christian anthropology even in its most extreme Calvinist forms. Another feature of human beings as understood by Christians is that they belong to one another in communities. Roman Catholic economic thinking has kept this point alive, and Christians in general believe that human beings are more adequately and realistically understood as persons-in-communities rather than as individuals-in-markets. From the Christian point of view, therefore, participation in a healthy community is more important to human well-being than consumption of goods and services beyond what are essential for biological health. But the notion of human community is absent from the economic model. As a result, economic theory has supported economic practice that has long been, and still is, engaged in an extended and global assault on human communities.

The most dramatic instances of this assault are to be found in what until recently we have called the Second and Third worlds. Communists were dedicated to destroying traditional communities of all sorts so as to attain a rational world oriented to efficient production and equality in consumption. Development models for the less-industrialized nations saw traditional community as a major obstacle; for example, the idea of community nurtured values that made workers reluctant to leave their people even when higher wages were available elsewhere. Thus, programs of development based on these models have in fact destroyed much of that community.

However, one need not look outside the United States to see how the economy, guided by the model sketched above, has assaulted community. Owners of factories are encouraged by the approved model to remain always alert to the possibility that their capital could be invested more profitably elsewhere. When such an opportunity is found, the theory declares it desirable that the factory be closed and the money be invested in another way. This mobility of capital keeps the economy as a whole growing. The destructive effects of factory closings on the communities in which they are located do not appear in the economic equations. Consideration of them is viewed as sentimentality that inhibits economic growth.

Rural America also illustrates the effects of the economic model. Since World War II the dominant economic theory as applied to U.S. agriculture has resulted in dramatically increased productivity—again, as measured by total product divided by hours of human labor. This has been achieved by specialization and mechanization, involving vastly increased use of fossil fuels, chemical fertilizers, pesticides, and herbicides, and vastly decreased labor. Farming thus has been reshaped according to the industrial model, and thousands of rural communities have been destroyed. This has resulted in mass migrations into the inner cities and suburban areas, where the quality of community established is likely to be inferior to what was destroyed in the countryside.

This example shows the intimate connection between the degradation of the biosphere and the destruction of human community. Small family farms were quite capable of degrading the earth; of that there is no question. But in many parts of the world they have operated in sustainable ways for millennia. In the United States, also, they could be reformed along sustainable lines. In any case, their use of exhaustible resources and their pollution of the environment were small in comparison to the factory farming that has replaced them. The Amish, for example, have shown that a far superior form of farming—both for the sake of human community and for the sake of the environment—is possible.

The above critique has been limited to two quite simple, and quite basic, points. Christians, in general, believe that the earth is God's and that to degrade it is evil, implying that as we structure our economic life we should aim to meet human needs without further degradation of the planet. Christians, in general, also believe that our relationships with one another are at least as important as our consumption of goods and services, implying that we should find ways of meeting our needs that do not continue to destroy human communities. Indeed, if we are persons-in-communities rather than individuals-in-markets, the goal of the economy should be the building up of communities rather than the expansion of markets.

These points may seem quite simple, but their implications are very radical. They require that Christians help envisage and implement a profoundly different economic order. Otherwise, the situation will continue much as in the past, when, almost regardless of avowed religious beliefs, economic practices led to the continuing despoliation of the earth. While this book does not provide a detailed blueprint of what the different economic order would be like, the two points above can help illustrate how it would differ from the one that embodies the presently dominant ideals.

First, placing economic activity in the context of the whole earth requires attention to the question of scale. Bigger is obviously not necessarily better, so the optimum scale of the human economy in relation to the total economy becomes basically a question of sustainability. When the effects of the economy on the environment undercut the possibility of its own continuance, the scale is too large.

The determination of the optimum scale of the global economy will inevitably have disturbing consequences, especially when viewed with now-dominant assumptions. Already the present scale of the economy is clearly unsustainable. Yet three-fourths of the world's people are extremely poor, and even the affluent fourth are far from satisfied with their present level of consumption. Very few are prepared to cut their consumption drastically in order to share with those who have more urgent needs. We seem to have no choice but to increase production greatly in order to respond to these needs.

The dilemma is a real and difficult one, but it is not wholly insuperable. The issue of scale needs to be formulated more exactly to examine not how many goods and services are available to people, but how much pressure the production of these goods and services places on the environment. Human ingenuity needs to be directed toward meeting more human needs with less disruptive impact on the environment. We are already making some progress in this direction. For example, automobiles and appliances can be designed to require far less energy without any reduction in service to the consumer. Houses can be built so as to require little or no energy for heating and cooling other than that from the sun. And crops can be grown organically with greatly reduced use of oil-based products.

Another, and essential, step in meeting more needs with less impact on the environment is shortening supply lines. Compare two scenarios for putting tomatoes on your dining table. In the first scenario, they have been machine-harvested, packaged, and shipped an average of twelve hundred miles. More energy goes into packaging and shipping them than into growing and harvesting, and the total environmental stress is considerable. In the extreme opposite scenario, you would raise tomatoes organically in your own garden. Any resultant environmental stress would be negligible, and one might even participate in the regeneration of the soil that is so badly needed. (I am not dwelling here on the superior taste and food value of the home-grown tomato.) Obviously there are intermediate scenarios. With produce bought at the local farmers' market or at roadside stands, much of the cost of packaging and shipping is eliminated, and often the tomatoes are grown in less energy-consumptive and soil-destructive ways.

Some of these means of providing goods in ways that place less pressure on the environment are in only modest tension with dominant economic theory. More efficient use of energy is often profitable to the companies that adopt new technologies for that purpose. Nevertheless, much of the progress that has been made, even at that level, has involved government intervention, and most of the rest has resulted from the committed work of persons who care for the whole earth enough to demonstrate the advantages of energy efficiency.[2] Left to themselves, those acting chiefly by the standard model have been slow to adopt the needed changes.

Advocacy of small family farms and shorter supply lines, on the other hand, directly opposes the implications drawn from the dominant model. These proposals, which shift the concern from the growth of the market to the well-being of the whole earth, will be rejected as long as that growth is the primary aim of policymakers. The contrast is especially clear between the goal of shortening supply lines and the now-dominant economic model, which calls for greater and greater specialization over larger and larger regions, making each region dependent on trade for most of its needs. Supply lines grow longer and longer. Costs of packaging and transportation increase and inevitably involve costs to the environment as well. The system is inherently unsustainable. The sustainable alternative is one in which smaller and smaller regions produce more and more of the goods they need closer and closer to where they are consumed. These economies will contribute little to the greenhouse effect and will survive the exhaustion of oil.

This leads directly to the second theological principle enunciated above in criticism of the dominant version of *Homo economicus.* Shorter supply lines mean more economic self-reliance and relative stability in smaller regions. Instead of economic forces breaking up community as at present, they would encourage it. Communities would have considerable power over their own economies rather than being at the mercy of distant deciders or impersonal market forces.

Indeed, from a Christian point of view, this is just as important a reason for redirecting the economy as is the concern for the earth. If people are more accurately understood as persons-in-community than as individuals-in-markets, then the economy should serve community rather than the growth of markets, even apart from the unsustainability of policies aimed at endless market growth. Healthy communities require that people through their communities have basic control over the means of livelihood, which is possible only when there are relatively self-sufficient economies in small regions.

People living in healthy communities may be less preoccupied with increased consumption. For example, when faced with a choice between more enjoyment of work and more goods and services, many of them may choose the former. There may be increased willingness in the First World to live more frugally so as to share the earth more fairly with others. Many people may find this different lifestyle more satisfying, and biblical teaching about possessions may take on a meaning it has almost lost in most of our churches. Thus, in addition to ordering society so that less pressure on the environment can accompany increasing production, we may have a society in which people measure their well-being less by their possessions and consumption and more by their contribution to the well-being of others.

The Christian teachings to which I have appealed thus far are simple and basic ones. They have been rhetorically present throughout Christian history. Unfortunately, in practical effect they have often been subordinated to other emphases. Especially since the Enlightenment, many Protestants have identified their faith with a very individualistic relation to God and to neighbor. The rest of creation has either dropped out of the picture, been viewed sentimentally, or been seen as a field of conquest. This form of Christianity has lent itself to cooperation with the dominant economic order and the theory that supports it.

For this reason, the fact that these teachings are simple and basic ones does not mean that the theological task of repentance and transformation is an easy one. The deep separation Protestants have often made between creation and redemption must be overcome. Without losing the important truth in individualism, Protestants must recover an authentic doctrine of the church and also of the wider human community. Without ceasing to appreciate the distinctiveness of human beings as made in the image of God, Protestants must overcome the modern dualism between human beings and the remainder of the created order that modern hermeneutics has imposed on the Bible. There is much work to be done.

Further, Protestants need to build on the best in the modern social teaching of the church. This teaching has called us to be responsible in and for the world, which has never been more important. We have learned not to impose simple ideals naively on complex situations but to analyze them thoroughly and then find ways to move toward Christian goals within them. Yet there has been a widespread movement in the church to reject those leaders who engage in such analysis of social issues. When they make pronouncements and take actions guided by that analysis, they are accused of imposing their private political views on the church. If we are to be responsible in relation to the global crisis, the church as a whole must commit itself to Christian thinking and to having its actions informed by that thinking. If instead we allow ourselves to be easily swayed by attractive slogans, our good intentions will be directed to ends that are at best harmless and too often supportive of the forces that are degrading the earth.

For example, we are inclined to celebrate interdependence. In our opposition to individualism and to nationalism, we affirm that we as individuals need one another and that nations, too, need one another, as we all need God. Interdependence is a central mark of healthy community. Hence, as economic development makes all dependent on others for survival, our immediate response is that this is a great gain.

The free trade that makes this possible seems equally admirable. However, careful analysis shows that interdependence as it develops out of free trade means the dependence of all on those who control the movement of capital and the terms of trade. They act according to the laws of the market, which dictate that they seek maximum profit. Meanwhile, decisions made thousands of miles away on the basis of quite impersonal principles can wreak havoc in a village, a city, or even a whole country.

On the other hand, people who participate together in a real human community experience a desirable form of interdependence. In such a community, everyone is concerned with the fate of all the others, and everyone shares in making the decisions that determine their fate. There are risks in depending even on such a community, but these are the risks that faith encourages. They are very different from the total surrender of personal control to the impersonal forces of the market.

Similarly, when we examine free trade carefully, we see that it is often not free at all. Companies are free to ignore national boundaries and the well-being of the people of the nation. But once whole peoples have become dependent on imports for their survival, they are no longer free *not* to trade. They must sell what they have at whatever price others set in order to import what they need. Trade is truly free only when those who trade are free to trade or not to trade. That is possible only when they are basically self-sufficient and can base their decisions on what truly benefits them. Christians can affirm and celebrate this kind of free trade. The global community we want is a community of free peoples, not the subordination of all to a few transnational corporations.

If the church finds it difficult to reform its own teaching and practice in light of some of its central convictions, how much more difficult will it be to seek a change in the direction of public policy and economic theory and practice? The ideal of free trade is deeply entrenched, while the ideal of relative self-reliance or self-sufficiency has a modest foothold at the fringes of Christian economic thinking. Even if Christians and other religious groups throw their support in this direction, they will still not win the day. But it may force a serious discussion that will show the futility of the effort to heal the world's sickness by more of the medicine that has already so degraded the planet.

When Christians think still more carefully about the world they should try to bring into being, other theological issues appear on which there is less unanimity. One of the most important is the relation of human beings to other species of animals, a topic of heated debate outside the church. Unfortunately, the church still avoids entering the discussion.

Much of this discussion today is polarized. The traditional Christian view is that only human beings are created in the image of God, are objects of divine redemptive activity, and should be objects of human ethical concern. In this view animals exist only for the sake of human beings, so that any use of animals for any human purpose is justified, whatever suffering is inflicted on the animals.

The same point is made by many ethical thinkers who derive their support from other than biblical sources. They hold that only human beings have intrinsic value and are objects of ethical concern, while other creatures have value only as they are priced in the market. This position may be based on the judgment that only humans are rational, or employ language, or have self-consciousness. All these claims are questionable.

In reaction to this established position, more and more thinkers and activists are asserting that rights should be based on sentience rather than rationality, the use of language, or self-consciousness. There is every indication that many animals are sentient, so their pleasure and pain are of ethical importance in just the same way as the pleasure or pain of a fellow human being. The conclusion is that the basic rights of human beings not to be caused avoidable suffering and not to be killed apply to all sentient animals.

The polarization occurs in part because the language of rights tends to be absolutistic. In much of the secular discussion, it seems that either one has the right to life or one does not. There are no degrees of rights. In this context, theologians have the possibility of bringing biblical perspectives and categories into play in ways that can be genuinely helpful to all.

The most influential accounts of the relation of human beings and other creatures are to be found in Genesis. Here God is depicted as having created all other creatures before human beings. God sees that they are good. In contemporary philosophical language, God sees that they have intrinsic value. There is nothing in the text to suggest that they have value only for human beings. Yet human beings *are* given dominion over all the others.

This double message is reinforced in the story of the Flood. Through the instrumentality of Noah, all the species are saved, but there is no indication that they are saved only because they are useful to him. Noah is obeying God's command, not calculating his own interests. After the Flood God makes a covenant, not with Noah alone, but with all the animals as well. In the biblical account, then, the other animals do have intrinsic value. They are objects of divine concern and should be objects of human ethical concern. But they do not have the same moral status as human beings, who are created in the image of God and given dominion over all the others.

Jesus also makes the general point that other animals have intrinsic value and that nevertheless God has special concern for human beings. He emphasizes that God cares about each individual sparrow. This is important. But the main point Jesus is making is that God cares more, much more, about human beings.

From the biblical perspective, the church has not been wrong to concentrate its attention heavily on human beings, but it *has* been wrong to neglect responsibility for the well-being of other creatures. The church is certainly wrong in not having developed ethical guidelines for the exercise of human dominion over other animals as it has developed guidelines for the exercise of dominion by some human beings over others. Finally, the church is scandalously slow in responding to the urgent issues now before the public with respect to experimentation on animals, cruel methods of producing meat, the slaughter of porpoises, and so forth. These *are* moral issues from the biblical point of view.

Some of these issues are separable from the question of the degradation of the earth. We could stop degrading the creation in general and still treat individual animals with great cruelty. Alternately, we could stop inhumane treatment of individual animals and continue degrading the creation. For this reason, it may seem inappropriate to raise these questions here.

On the other hand, the way we understand the relation of human beings and other species does have an effect on envisioning the world toward which we should work as Christians. To put the matter simply, should we strive for a world that has as many people as can be supported in a decent way regardless of what this means for other species? Or should our goal be a world in which the human species restricts its population so that viable populations of other species also can flourish? Practically this means, should Christians work to maintain and expand wilderness? Or as human need for more land grows with rising population, can we regard wilderness as expendable?

Those who adopt the latter position argue from the commandment to Adam and Eve to be fruitful and multiply, along with the gift of dominion. Since no limit is set on human multiplying, it is argued, other species must be destroyed when their habitat is needed by human beings. People then would preserve other species only when they are likely to be of significant benefit to human beings.

However, when the texts are read more carefully, another meaning seems to come forward. Other creatures were also given the command to be fruitful and multiply. There is no indication that giving the same command to human beings abrogates the earlier commandment. Thus, human dominion should be so exercised as to provide space for other species to share the planet. The clear indication of God's concern to save all species, as told in the story of the Flood, confirms this message. In contemporary terms, biodiversity is important to God.

Returning to the language of the earlier part of the chapter, one can say that the community to which human beings belong extends beyond humanity. In the Jewish scriptures the relation to the land is centrally important. Separation from the land impoverishes our humanity. The full community includes not only human beings but the biosphere as well. An economy acceptable to Christians today will be one that sustains and regenerates this whole community.

Thus far I have stayed close to widely accepted biblical and traditional teachings. This is important. Collective repentance depends on the clarity of the message and its clear Christian authority. Nevertheless, in conclusion, I want to take another, more controversial, step, one that is based on biblical passages, but that must argue against the dominant theological tradition.

I affirm a panentheistic view of the relation of God and the world that has gained ground in recent theology. Many theologians have moved in this direction recognizing that the emphasis on God's transcendence alone is not faithful to the Bible and neglects actual Christian experience. I also believe that this shift will deepen Christian concern for the earth and all its creatures.[3]

Panentheism reacts most strongly and decisively against deism, which thinks of God as external to the world and of the world as external to God. My emphasis here will be on the second form of externality. Some of the language of the Bible supports this way of thinking, and it became dominant in later Christianity due to the way in which philosophical ideas were introduced into Christian theology. In particular, the Greeks thought of the Divine as unchanging and therefore unaffected by what happened in the changing world. Divine immutability thus came to be a standard Christian doctrine.

The idea that what happens in the world makes no difference to God was hard to reconcile with the Bible. Aristotle consistently interpreted this as meaning that God does not know what happens in the world, but Christians could not follow him there. Probably the most influential solution was to argue that God knows all temporal events nontemporally. Thus God's life includes knowledge of worldly events, but this knowledge is immutable, since all the events, past, present, and future from the human point of view, are alike present eternally for God.

In this limited sense, the world has been held to be present in God even in this classical tradition. Nevertheless, the emphasis remained on God's separateness and transcendence. Even though God knows what happens in the world, it has been said, God is not affected by these events. God's perfect blessedness is neither enriched by human joy nor disturbed by human suffering. This doctrine has led to a considerable shift of religious attention away from God and toward Jesus and Mary as those who could be believed to care in a real way.

Panentheism argues, instead, that all that happens in the created order enters fully into the divine life. God's knowledge of our lives is not abstract but fully concrete. God rejoices with us in our joy and suffers with us in our pain. God experiences with us the difference between what is past, what is present, and what is future. Our decisions affect the life of God as well as our fellow creatures. This doctrine heightens our sense of the importance of what happens to the earth. What we do to the least of our fellow creatures we do also to God. When we degrade the earth, we deny to God the full richness of experience God might otherwise have. When we kill off whole species, the potentiality for the divine life is impoverished.

This does not mean that God's life is in our hands. God is everlasting, and all that has ever been remains, and will always remain, part of God's life. We can take nothing away. But the exact character of God's present and future experience is affected by what we do. And this is as true of what we do to other animals and to the earth itself as of what we do to other human beings.

The Christian who accepts this vision as more faithful to the biblical witness than the deism it seeks to replace cannot remain easy with the continuation of present practices. The suffering we are imposing on other creatures and on our human descendants we are imposing on the God who so loved us as to freely suffer on our behalf. If we can cease to add to the divine suffering only by personal sacrifice, the willingness to make such sacrifices will seem an appropriate response to God's gifts to us.

2
Economics and
the Humanities

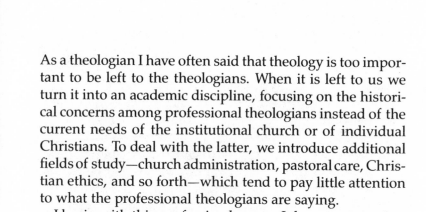

As a theologian I have often said that theology is too important to be left to the theologians. When it is left to us we turn it into an academic discipline, focusing on the historical concerns among professional theologians instead of the current needs of the institutional church or of individual Christians. To deal with the latter, we introduce additional fields of study—church administration, pastoral care, Christian ethics, and so forth—which tend to pay little attention to what the professional theologians are saying.

I begin with this confession because I do not want to imply that the academic discipline of economics is the only area with problems. Similar problems affect philosophy, the study of literature, and even history. To whatever extent we humanists succeed by the university norms for academic disciplines, we generate our topics for investigation internally. The needs of the wider public, even of our students, become secondary to the demands of the discipline. The study of the humanities becomes less and less genuinely humane.

Because I am a theologian, I have given a theological

name to this devotion to disciplines. I view it as a form of idolatry. In modern theological parlance, idolatry means according ultimate loyalty to what is not worthy of such loyalty. We speak of bibliolatry, for example, when people give ultimate loyalty to the Bible.

In the university scholars are strongly encouraged to be completely devoted, at least so far as their professional life is concerned, to the advancement of their discipline. I call this *disciplinolatry.* Service to the university, students, and the wider public is often secondary to this commitment. To use less theological language, I could say that this is a matter of priorities, and that the ethos of the university encourages us to distort our priorities. Lifelong study of literature, for example, should be for the sake of enriching public appreciation of literature rather than of advancing an academic discipline. If that were the case, scholars would be attentive to the use and response to literature in the broader public and would be asking how they could teach in such a way as to improve tastes and increase enjoyment. But questions of this sort are usually left to the pedagogues, whose work is viewed with some disdain.

In the very long run the harm done by disciplinolatry in the humanities may be more serious than that done by disciplinolatry in the social sciences. But at the moment, the most urgent task is to counter its effects in the latter and especially in economics. Economists, as a group, are not any worse than the rest of us, but their work has a more direct effect on public policy. The basic directions taken by both Democratic and Republican administrations in the United States are far more affected by the guidance of economists than by any influence exerted by humanists.

Economics has not always played this leading role. And because one of the contributions that humanists can make to public affairs is historical perspective, let me suggest a sweeping view of the past millennium in terms of the primary concerns of the body politic. Obviously, I grossly

simplify complex matters, but there is a place for such sim-
plifications. My mentor, Alfred North Whitehead, com-
mented that it is more important that a proposition be
interesting than that it be true, but that truth adds to interest.[1] If what is initially interesting does not have some illuminating relation to reality, then it quickly loses interest. I
hope that the periodization of history that I propose has
enough relation to the facts to sustain interest.

In the first half of this millennium the body politic focused on honor. Sometimes wars were fought to avoid dis-
honor to princes. Of course, wealth and power were closely
connected to honor, but it was not honorable to seek these
as ends in themselves. Even more important than the honor
due to princes was the honor due to God. Religious concerns were primary. The Crusades are the clearest instance
of wars justified by religion, but they were not the only
ones. Further, many of the decisions governing the lives of
peoples were made, or at least justified, in relation to what
was required by God.

Both the intensity and the divisiveness of religious feeling climaxed in the Reformation and its aftermath. In the
seventeenth century, Europe was plunged into a bloodbath
by religious zeal. This led to a widespread reaction in public opinion. Instead of forcing religious conformity on all, it
seemed far better to most thoughtful people to allow each
political unit to decide on its own religious institutions and
beliefs. This policy was instituted in central Europe by the
Peace of Westphalia in 1648.

The most effective political units at this time were
nation-states, some of which found ways to allow equal
treatment of diverse religious groups within their own borders. In any case, the focus of concern shifted from religion
to the political unit, from seeking to honor a ruler to more
practical questions of national independence, national
power, and national prosperity. Nationalism thus super-

seded religion as the unifying devotion of most European peoples.

The problem with such a periodization, of course, is that nationalism can be traced to earlier periods, while both religion and human honor continued to play a large role in the later period. Whether careful sociological study of Europeans in the eighteenth century would support the view that nationalism superseded religious commitments for more than half of them is doubtful. While I am not making that kind of a claim, I am suggesting that there was a gradual but profound shift. People in Europe were far less interested in fighting wars of religion and far more willing to give their lives for their nations.

It is important to emphasize that such a periodization is irrelevant to much of the world. Today religion plays an enormously important role, especially in the Muslim world. Islamic nations have on the whole less appeal to their people than does Islam. In other instances, such as in Israel and Northern Ireland, the nationalist and religious feelings are inseparable. Still, in Europe and in its extension in North America, nationalism took over the functions once exercised by Christianity as determining the primary functions of the body politic.

What I have said thus far may impress you as more true than interesting. That is, you may find it fairly obvious. But I now propose that a second great shift has occurred, one that has been less clearly highlighted.

Just as the excesses of the seventeenth-century religious wars led to a revulsion against absolutizing particular religious convictions and commitments, so the excesses of nationalism that eventuated in World War II have undercut its convincing power. Nazism is the caricature of nationalism, and the revulsion against its explicit absolutization of race and nation has made it impossible for nationalism to continue as the supreme loyalty of people in the North Atlantic. This is especially apparent in Europe, where the nations have been busily surrendering elements of their sovereignty. Much of the loyalty once directed to France or Germany is now directed to Europe. Yet it would be a mistake to see this as simply an extension of national feeling to the continent as a whole.

If we ask what has superseded nationalism in Europe, the answer is not continentalism. It is *economism*. What the Europeans have constructed is the European *Economic* Community. For the sake of greater prosperity for all, French, Germans, and Italians are willing to make profound changes in their societies. In this way they believe they can collectively be more competitive with the other great centers of economic power. Few fear that a European army will attempt to add to the glory of Europe by conquering new territories. But there is plenty of reason to anticipate that European capital and goods may dominate markets in many parts of the world.

The shift to economism is in process in the United States as well, although it was partly masked by the cold war. That war could be viewed in nationalistic terms, and no doubt there were such elements in it. But even then the argument was that we must oppose the Soviet Union primarily because of its economic system.

The continuing tension between the nationalism of our recent past and the emerging economism was manifest in the recent war with Iraq. Everyone knew that control of the oil wealth of the Persian Gulf was at the heart of our involvement there. But it was important to put the issue in terms of the national integrity of Kuwait and the threat to that of Saudi Arabia. As a people we are not quite ready to acknowledge that we go to war for primarily economic reasons. Also, the enormous, even absurd, rejoicing over our easy victory was an expression of national feeling. We could be proud once again of our national power and prowess. And we were pleased that we got other nations to finance our war.

Despite the continuing strength of nationalism in the United States, the primary determinant of national policies today is economics. Except in matters of war, we quite openly assert this. Policies are deemed good if they prevent depressions and keep the economy growing. The electorate rewards administrations that are successful in this regard or that happen to be in power when market forces are working well. Occasionally other issues arise that appeal to noneconomic commitments, such as abortion or health care for the poor, but they are treated as special interest concerns. Preoccupation with the economy as a whole is not thought of in this way.

Of course, the economic strength of the nation has been a concern of nationalism all along. Hence, the focus of all administrations since World War II on this characteristic may be a continuation of the nationalism we have known for centuries, not an indication that there has been a great shift from nationalism to economism in our society. However, the evidence for this shift is clearer in the deep commitment of recent administrations to free trade.

A nation pursuing free trade when it already has an industrial and trade advantage may be simply seeking to maintain its national advantage. But the commitment of the Reagan and Bush administrations, continued by President Clinton, came at a time when, viewed in terms of our country's national interest, free trade is not an obvious boon. One may argue that these administrations would not pursue free trade so vigorously if they were not convinced that it promotes national interests, and that may be true at some level. But the argument is consistently made in economic terms, not national ones. This assumption, that the national good is measured by economic growth, is what I am calling economism.

Even though economism does not dominate the spirituality of all peoples, it is the "religion" that governs planetary affairs. After World War II the United Nations was

created as an inter*national* body and has played a significant role in world affairs. But the less-noticed institutions—the World Bank, the International Monetary Fund,
and the General Agreement on Tariffs and Trade—have
had more effect on the day-to-day lives of people everywhere, and power continues to move from the United Nations to these economic agencies. A major reason is that in
the United Nations discussions are public, and at least in
the assembly they involve participation from many of the
world's peoples. In the economic institutions, much discussion goes on secretly, and nations with greater economic
power have more control.

It is significant also that when the leaders of the world's
great powers gather for an annual discussion, trying to
work through problems that have arisen among them, the
meetings are called "economic summits." The major problems with which they must deal are assumed to be economic ones. Their meetings are far more closely connected
with the international economic agencies mentioned in the
preceding paragraph than with the issues dealt with in the
United Nations Assembly.

When nations and international agencies are committed
to economism, they obviously will turn for guidance to
professional economists, who are thought to know most
about the economy and who have professional expertise in
enabling the economy to grow. These professional economists are the products and leaders of the academic discipline of economics. Thus, an examination of the discipline
to which they give so much devotion is especially important to all of us whose fate is in their hands. If its limitations
are as serious as those of our own disciplines, we have
reason to be alarmed about any direct application of its
findings to the real world.

My judgment is that, indeed, the limitations of economics are analogous to the limitations of other academic disci-

plines. Like them, it is based on a series of abstractions.
Like them, it tends to forget what has been abstracted from
and to apply its findings to the real world as if nothing of
importance had been left out. This is what Whitehead
called the fallacy of misplaced concreteness. While this fallacy is widespread throughout academia, the instances in
economics are today most threatening to our global future.[2]

Economic theory is based, as it should be, on a model of
the human being. Any such model must abstract from the
full concreteness of actual human beings. To point out that
the economic model, *Homo economicus*, is such an abstraction, is not a criticism. Further, the first test of any such abstraction is its fruitfulness, and the economic model passes
this test with flying colors.

The criticism implied in accusing economics of commit-
ting the fallacy of misplaced concreteness is that the academic discipline encourages its practitioners to neglect the
degree of abstractness of their model. When they apply
conclusions drawn from the model to the real world, economists should remember what has been abstracted from
and ask whether the application does violence to elements
of reality that have not been considered in the development
of the theory. If this violence is occasional and can be ad-
justed for, this subsequent taking into account of the neglected elements may suffice. If the violence is pervasive,
then the model itself needs revision. The criticism of economics is that the abstraction involved at the base of its theory is almost entirely ignored, and that those whose
thought is most fully formed by the discipline do not pay
attention to the violence their recommended policies do to
real people and to the rest of nature.

The academic discipline of economics, like my own discipline and many others, takes its problems from its own
past history and not from the effects of its application in the
real world. To put this in another way, these effects, when
considered at all, are viewed through the categories of the

discipline in such a way that many of them go unnoticed. Accordingly, it is important that people from other fields and disciplines evaluate the effects of the application of economic theory to the world. Negative consequences that are being ignored by economists should be brought into interdisciplinary conversation with a view to modifying the basic model.

A more concrete criticism of economic theory is that it abstracts from a great many features of human beings. Indeed, the only motive of human action that is included in *Homo economicus* is self-interest. When we observe ourselves in our roles of buying and selling, the model seems accurate enough. We are always seeking the best prices we can for what we sell and the best bargains we can find when we shop. Because this model describes our behavior so well, economics has been brilliantly successful in describing what happens in the market and in recommending ways to make the market more effective.

Yet human beings do not function *only* in the way predicted by the model, even in relation to all economic activity. Other motives play a role. For example, people give money to causes in which they believe. Economists try hard, but unsuccessfully, to incorporate this fact into their models. One way of doing this is to say that our actions necessarily express what we perceive as our self-interest when we take them. To cite another example, strong empirical evidence shows that a sense of fairness plays a large role in actual human behavior, including economic behavior. But the calculations with which economists work are based on a much narrower definition of self-interest and not on careful observation of real actions.

Steven E. Rhoads offers a fascinating account of the relation of economics and fairness in *The Economist's View of the World*. A political scientist with broad humanistic sensitivities, Rhoads immersed himself in economics for a decade. His report is balanced, praising economics for many of its accomplishments, but also noting its shortcomings. Rhoads reports on experiments such as the following:

> [L]arge groups of people are given tokens they can invest either in an individual exchange that returns 1 cent per token to the individual investing, or in a group exchange that returns 2.2 cents per token but divides these earnings among everyone in the group regardless of who invests. In other words, in the group exchange, the subject receives a share of the return on his own investment (if any) and the same share of the return on the investment in the group exchange made by the other group members. Most economists would predict that a self-interested individual would put nothing in the group exchange because this behavior maximizes benefits to himself. . . . But, in fact, in a number of experiments people have voluntarily contributed substantial resources—usually between 40 and 60 percent—to the group exchange. . . . Many in the experiments have also said that a "fair" person would contribute even more than they did. The only notable exception has been a group of entering graduate students in economics. They contributed only 20 percent, found the concept of fairness alien, and were only half as likely to indicate that they were concerned with fairness in making their decision.[3]

Rhoads reports that economists commenting on this data assumed that the players must be ignorant of their own best interest.

While this example is trivial in itself, it highlights aspects of reality from which the economists' model abstracts. Further, the response of economists shows the extent of their tendency to ignore, or even deny, that which the model omits. Far more important are studies of voting that indicate many people consistently support policies—such as programs for the aged that will cost them money—which are not in their own best interest as economists conceive this. The danger, of course, is that, consistently viewing the world as economists are trained to see it affects the actual motivation of those who do so. And in an economistic society, an increasing number of people will be socialized to accept as normative what economists call rational behavior.

One other careful study of the anthropology underlying economic theory, by scholars from another discipline, is *The Individual in the Economy: A Survey of Economic Psychology*, by three psychologists, Stephen E. G. Lea, Roger M. Tarpy, and Paul Webley.[4] Among many other topics, they determine that the economic axiom of insatiability—that is, that human wants are without limit and can, therefore, never be satisfied—which is derived from the economic model and important to economic theory, is empirically in error.

What troubles me most about economic theory is that it abstracts from the social or communal character of human existence and fails to notice that it does so. Underlying its neglect of motives other than self-interest is a radically individualistic view of human beings. It proposes that *Homo economicus* is self-enclosed, that is, unaffected by relations to others. This model arose in the late eighteenth century and reflected the individualism of the period. The fact that it continues to control economic thought despite the changes that have taken place in other disciplines and in the cultural sensitivity as a whole is a mark of the way academic disciplines develop—that is, again, out of their own internal histories rather than in relation to the realities of the world of thought or even to empirical facts.

Most of us today believe (I am even inclined to say "know") that human beings do not exist in isolation. We are largely constituted by our social relations. The health of the community in which we participate is crucial to our own well-being. We are persons-in-community rather than isolated individuals unaffected by our relations to others.

The theories developed by economists and applied to the real world ignore this aspect of the human situation. The science of economics aims to make more goods available, to increase consumption. In general, it finds established communities an impediment to that arrangement of individuals that is most productive, and so exerts a strong pressure in favor of policies that are destructive of community. The impact of these policies in our own country and especially in the less-industrialized world has been enormous and, in my opinion, disastrous.

Central, bureaucratic planning offers no improvement here with respect to the effects on community. If anything, it is more destructive. Socialist theory, at least in its Marxist form, had no more interest in community than did its capitalist enemy. And Marxist societies have been even more ruthless than capitalist ones in the destruction of traditional communities.

What is the alternative? In my view, the issue is the optimum size of the market. The local markets that existed in the eighteenth century when Adam Smith formulated what has become modern economic theory did not destroy community. They operated within established communities and served them. But a national market on the scale of that in the United States does destroy local communities. It encourages the movement of capital around the market with labor following capital.

The argument for the larger market, as discussed in chapter 1, is that this allows specialization, and specialization is the key to productivity. But specialization weakens local community in a second way. Instead of developing a self-sustaining economy, a community specializes in producing one thing, primarily for export to other parts of the market. Since it can produce more of this one thing than it could produce of the many things it needs, it is in position to buy more of the other products from other centers specializing in their production. Hence, measured in terms of resultant consumption, the community is improved. Of course, it is radically dependent on those who control its specialized production, since apart from this it cannot sustain itself at all. Usually those who control this production live elsewhere and decide how long to maintain production at this location by proper economic considerations, that is, how long this is the most profitable investment of capital.

In the past two decades we have seen the increasing effects of the global market on both local communities and the national economy as a whole. Thus far, this global market is hemmed in by many restrictions. But the U.S. government, both Republican and Democratic administrations, have been committed to reducing and ultimately removing these restrictions in hopes of producing a single, global free market. This is the utopian aim of economism.

From what is this free market or free trade free? The national free market is free from restrictions by states or local communities. The global free market is to be free from restrictions by national governments as well. It will make possible still higher degrees of specialization and will further discourage efforts of local communities or nations to supply most of their own needs. Capital will move freely throughout the world to those places where it can be most profitably invested. Labor, which cannot move as freely, will be at an increasing disadvantage.

The tension between this economistic utopia and the nationalism that still lingers is apparent. National governments are asked to surrender their right to control their national economies. The basic control passes into the hands of the owners of capital who move their investments around the world to take advantage of opportunities to improve their profit margins. Full realization of the economistic utopia will destroy the significance of national boundaries completely with respect to any aspect of public policy that affects the economy. This entails an enormous reduction of national authority. The reward is that the global economy will grow more rapidly, and the hope is that most people in most nations will participate in that growth. However, this hope is *not* supported by historical experience.

While my greatest concern about academic economics is that it abstracts from the communal character of human existence, it must be understood that this communal character extends beyond the relations to other human beings to include relations to the wider world. For the dominant economic theory, human beings do function as ends, that is, the goal is to improve human economic well-being as measured by production and consumption of goods and services. The effects on other creatures are of no importance. They are treated only under the heading of land or natural resources, and these are viewed as commodities valued only by the prices paid for them in the market.

Actually the situation is worse than this suggests. It would be possible to view other creatures only as resources for human use and yet recognize their exhaustibility. But economic theory treats natural resources in general as unlimited. Economists point out that as certain resources have become scarce, advances in technology have made more of that resource available or have produced substitutes.

Here again, theories abstracted from one range of events are viewed as having universal applicability without much empirical examination. The fallacy of misplaced concreteness is at work in very damaging ways. Because they are convinced that shortage of resources is not a problem, to state the matter minimally, traditional economists are generally among the last to propose policies of conservation.

Again, let me illustrate with a recent example. Amory and Hunter Lovins have taken the lead in pointing out that more efficient use of energy could allow us to have all the end-use we now have while reducing the consumption of resources.[5] For example, simply by using more efficient electrical fixtures, we could light our homes just as brightly with one-fourth of the present energy use. Aided by the Lovinses, many electrical utility companies have recognized that they can make better profits by subsidizing the shift of their customers to more energy-efficient appliances. This is cheaper than building new production facilities. Saving this money enables the utilities to provide electricity to customers at lower rates.

The same general principles apply to the use of gasoline. If cars averaged fifty miles to the gallon, we could drive just as much but exhaust fewer resources and reduce pollution. As long as requirements are placed equally on all auto manufacturers, their opportunities for profits are not reduced. The time when they will have to abandon the internal combustion engine is postponed. Automakers in this country have been much less willing to make these energy-conserving moves than utility companies. Nevertheless, it is in their long-term interest to support this approach.

One would think that a move so universally advantageous would be a cornerstone of any national energy policy. But most of the steps the federal government could take to promote more efficient use of energy were rejected by both the Reagan and the Bush administrations. Part of the reason is, of course, the political power of particular economic interests. But I believe the deeper answer is that the dominant economic theory does not support this approach. According to that theory, our well-being is a function of total production or consumption. To light our homes equally well with less electricity, or to drive our cars just as far with less gas, shows up as reduced production and consumption on the economists' charts.

The *Denver Post* ran an article on this topic featuring the achievements of Amory and Hunter Lovins in persuading business that its interest lay in using energy more efficiently.[6] Although the tone of the article was generally laudatory, the concluding paragraphs turned to negative comments. Reagan's secretary of energy, James Edwards, asserted that we cannot conserve ourselves into prosperity. The implication, of course, is that only growth in production, and hence increased use of resources, can make us prosperous.

The article continued:

> Lately, critics of greater support for energy efficiency voice worry over the economic disruption they say would inevitably come with change—particularly if conservation is prodded by such government moves as tightening vehicle fuel-economy standards. "We need a national energy policy that is aimed at getting on with the job of producing more oil and gas at home, to turn the wheels of industry and agriculture," Sen. Phil Gramm, a Republican from oil-rich Texas, said in a recent television interview. "Conservation has got to be part of it, too," Gramm said. "But we need a balanced policy, and we can't act as if just simply passing a law saying that we'll raise energy standards on cars to 40 miles a gallon isn't costly. Such a change would cost tens of billions of dollars, hundreds of thousands of jobs."[7]

The suggestion in the *Post* is that Gramm's reasons for opposing energy-efficiency as a major element of energy policy stem from the interests of Texas. Of course, that may be partly true. But I believe that they follow more from the fact that he is a first-rate economist. I assume that the billions of dollars of cost are really the reduced gross national product (GNP) resulting from using less oil. If the "wheels of industry and agriculture" are turned equally well with less gas and oil, the GNP will go down. Economists assume that if that happens, there will be fewer jobs. Because their only acceptable solution to unemployment is more rapid growth of the economy, they conclude that using energy more efficiently will cost jobs.

Given the present dominant economic theory and its application, growth is essential to the economy, and most of the steps needed for the survival of a healthy planet are perceived as threats to that. Yet for our very survival we urgently need an economy that meets human needs but uses fewer resources. The academic discipline of economics as now constituted does not help.

The question then is one of national purposes and goals. When we were nationalists, we could see the goal as a strong America able to defend itself against foreign interference and to impose its will throughout the Western Hemisphere. Of course, that spirit of nationalism is not dead. But I am suggesting that more determinative of national policy today is economism, the commitment to increase production and consumption of goods and services, and the subordination of other concerns to this end.

Humanists in general, and theologians in particular, should have something to say about purposes and goals. Most of us, I hope, do not favor either national power or increased GNP as the ultimate goal of national policy. But are we able to offer an alternative?

For the most part we have not done so. We have immersed ourselves in our several academic disciplines and ignored the larger questions of national policy and direction. We have supported some programs, such as the National Endowment for the Humanities, against the objections of economists. To do so, we must, as a group, argue that some forms of cultural expression are inherently better than others, and that this superiority cannot be determined by how much people are willing to pay for them. Economists, as a group, disapprove this activity, believing that there is no measure of value other than the prices set in the market. Thus far we have persuaded the government to maintain some support for the arts and humanities despite the objections of economists. Since this is so small a part of the national budget, economists reconcile themselves to this exercise in what they view as unjustified snobbery.[8]

Apart from such peripheral projections of our interests into the national agenda, our role is very small indeed. Yet so very much is at stake. The world is being reshaped before our eyes according to economistic principles. Although their application has saved us from the excesses of nationalism, it is leading us to disaster far faster than did the religious and nationalist ideals that economism has superseded. It is very important that humanists join the discussion of the proper goals and purposes of national policy—and soon.

For my own part I see no possibility or desirability in returning to either the religious or the nationalistic commitments of the past. I affirm the religious tolerance within each nation made possible by the rise of nationalism, and also the weakening of nationalism involved in economism. Still it seems a matter of almost ultimate importance that we not carry through the economistic system with its destruction of human communities and of the environment.

Is there an alternative? I believe that there is one alternative that is emerging among and within us that may function as an effective check on economism and eventually supersede it in a hopeful way. I will call this alternative *earthism*.

During the past twenty-five years there has been an upsurge of deep feeling about this planetary home of ours. This feeling taps into ancient sources still alive in the dim recesses of our unconscious. It finds support in many of the traditions that the West has long been suppressing and gains strength from the internal criticism of the West and the loss of power of its historic ideals. The picture of the earth from outer space, the one living planet, is its great symbol.

As a Christian theologian I cannot give *ultimate* support to earthism. This planet is not God. Yet devotion to the planet in most cases today leads to much the same action as devotion to God. It is *far* better than devotion to a particular religion, to a nation, or to the increase of economic production!

My contention is that today only earthism can function

as a unifying center of a healthy and desirable opposition to economism. Only it can generate the passion and energy, the level of commitment, that is needed. Traditional religions are recognizing the need to reemphasize their positive teachings about the earth in ways that can give needed support. Many people who find the older formulations irrelevant to their own experience and need resonate to ideas about their connectedness to the earth and all its creatures. Earth Day is the ritual celebration of the new sensibility.

The first great opportunity for earthism to attempt to affect global affairs was at the 1992 United Nations Earth Summit at Rio de Janeiro. Enormous amounts of background work had been done, much of it by earthists, who presented well-reasoned proposals to implement some of their agenda. The way was prepared also by *Our Common Future*, the report of the commission led by Gro Brundtland and usually called the *Brundtland Report*, which dealt realistically with the matrix of environmental crises confronting humanity.[9] It introduced of the idea that development must be sustainable and was widely accepted, at least rhetorically.

In spite of these advances, economism won the day. Indeed, it was never seriously challenged. The *Brundtland Report* called for development in the form of growth, a great deal more growth. Although its emphasis on greater efficiency and care in the use of resources is welcome, even this is not accepted by some devotees of economism. But the report challenged none of the fundamental assumptions of economism. Instead, it optimistically and unconvincingly proposed that we can function in an economistic way and still attain sustainability.

The real debate at Rio was between those who believed that we can protect some parts of the earth from further ravages without slowing down economic growth and those who feared that any significant efforts to protect the earth would inhibit the engines of growth. Since President Bush belonged to this second group, the United States blocked most of the significant actions that were proposed. To what extent the Clinton administration will renew the positive initiatives of Rio remains to be seen.

The question now is whether earthism can muster its devotees to a direct confrontation with economism. Thus far it has opposed particular actions that follow from economic theory, but it has generally not challenged the fundamental assumptions of economics. Or it has placed itself at such a distance from serious economic thinking as to be easily ignored. But simply pointing out the limitations of contemporary economic thinking will not suffice. Serious reflection on the economy is vital and involves positive proposals. An economic theory supportive of earthism should be worked out in some of the detail and rigor that characterize the current theory supportive of economism.

It is my belief that a new discussion is now beginning, one that seriously engages economists and the assumptions that shape their work and policy proposals.[10] Among those who are most deeply committed to the earth, a consensus is emerging about the political economy we need. It calls for relatively self-sufficient local economies as preferable to global economic integration into a single market. But this preference must not be presented as an alternative utopia. Today our concern should be for a decent and livable survival, not for a perfect society. Self-sufficient local economies encourage more stable communities, and stable communities are indispensable contexts for bringing up healthy children. But stable communities can be oppressive in all kinds of ways.

An interdependent global economy will reduce the power of everyone except a few manipulators of capital. The result will be not only oppressive but also profoundly dehumanizing for most of the world's people. It will increase the gap between the rich and the poor and hasten the exhaustion of resources and the pollution of the environment.

On the other hand, relatively self-sufficient local economies will make it possible for local communities to make most of the decisions that determine their destiny. But they will not ensure that these decisions will be just or wise. As a theologian who takes human sinfulness seriously, I am quite sure that many terrible things will take place in relatively self-sufficient local communities. I do not believe that any organization of society will put an end to injustice and stupidity.

The fact that a world based on local self-sufficiency will be a very imperfect world does not mean that it should not be sought. Although people who have some control over their own lives and destinies often use this power badly, it is still far better that they have such control than that they be pawns in the hands of distant manipulators of capital. Local communities can struggle for justice and liberation with at least some prospects of success. Also the rate of exhaustion of resources will be slowed, and the pressure on communities to move toward sustainable economies will be increased.

In our world, what takes place in one locality affects others. If all political power devolved to local communities, it might well be used in ways that are destructive of their neighbors and of the planetary future. Hence localism must be combined with federalism. Larger geographical units should be conceived as communities of communities and as communities of communities of communities of communities—on up to the global level. Determining the distribution of power among these levels is a complex task—and a necessary one.

The scope of the problem is primarily the issue here. Global warming can only be dealt with globally; so power to control some aspects of local economies, such as their contribution to the greenhouse effect, must be invested in a global body. Issues of acid rain can probably be dealt with at a continental level. The sustainability of agricultural practices can be dealt with more locally.

But the distribution of power at different levels can also help to check the worst abuses of power that may arise in local communities. Certain standards of human rights may be established globally, so that their violation can be restricted at every level. Local governments may be prevented from excluding minorities from participation. Once we give up hope for a utopian solution, we may devise systems of checks and balances that limit the destructive consequences of human sin and stupidity.

My purpose has not been to spell out the details of a global economy that has a chance of offering an attractive future. I have attempted to show that humanists in general, and theologians in particular, have a contribution to make. We can set the present dominance of economic considerations in historical perspective, thus relativizing it and opening the way to change. We can analyze and critique entrenched assumptions of economic theory and participate in describing the kind of society we favor.

The task is urgent. The pursuit of economic growth daily destroys human and environmental resources badly needed for a healthy future. To continue business as usual in our several disciplines while this destruction continues is profoundly irresponsible. May we awaken from our disciplinary slumbers before it is too late.

3

Sustainability
and Community

For more than a century the world has been taught that the great choice is between capitalism and socialism. Now capitalism has won the struggle in terms both of public power and human loyalties. It seems that it is time for rejoicing.

However, during the last quarter of a century, many people have realized that capitalism and socialism have not really been so very different. They are two sects in a larger quasi-religious movement based on commitment to economic growth as the organizing principle of personal and social life and as the basis for dealing with all the important problems of humanity.

Capitalism has sought growth through the reduction of social restrictions on individual initiative. Enormous disparities in wealth and power are accepted as an integral part of the system that most efficiently increases the total amount of goods and services. It has taught that impersonal market forces lead to the greatest efficiency in the allocation of resources and thus to the most rapid growth.

Socialism has held that the task of government is to encourage, manage, and direct growth for the sake of the people as a whole. It has undertaken to distribute the products of labor so that all will benefit to a more equal degree. All this is to be attained by planning on the part of those best able to understand and shape the entire process.

Socialist ideas, translated into practice, mean bureaucratic management. The professional advancement of individual bureaucrats turns out to have little correlation with the success of their economic policies or their management skills. Hence bureaucratic control does not lead to wise allocation of resources. Further, it is now clear that the impersonal mechanisms of the market deal with the complex problems of allocation of resources far more effectively than could the most conscientious and diligent bureaucrat. Also, the removal of the profit motive reduces the incentives to work hard and implement efficient procedures. In short, capitalism wins easily in the contest to see who can grow fastest.

We can all rejoice that the outcome was settled by relative success with respect to the shared goal of economic growth rather than by mutual destruction through nuclear weapons. Also, the end of the cold war is leading to some reduction in the portion of global resources used for military purposes. I trust this trend will go much further, and we can all greet this shift with enthusiasm. I have no desire to be a spoiler at the celebration.

Nevertheless, along with the celebration we need a healthy dose of realism. If the world is to be dominated by a false religion, it is better to have it unified than divided into sects whose mutual enmity endangers all life on the earth. But if the religion is false, its monolithic character does not save us from the destructive consequences of its errors. This is how the situation appears to those of us who believe that economic growth is a false god, an idol. The true options are not two forms of devotion to this false god. They are between worship of this false god and worship of the true God.

In understanding what is implied in the worship of the true God, the reflections of the World Council of Churches are illuminating. Its goal was long expressed to promote a just and participatory society rather than economic growth. As awareness of the ecological crisis dawned, there was growing realization that something was missing from this formulation. Margaret Mead proposed that the word *sustainable* be added, and this proposal was accepted at the Nairobi Assembly in 1975, so that the approved goal became "a just, participatory, and sustainable society." To me, as to the World Council of Churches, it seems that devotion to the true God requires that we commit ourselves to ordering our personal and institutional lives in just, participatory, and sustainable ways.

The norm of sustainability has direct relevance for economics. In contrast with the ideology of growth, an ideology of sustainability has developed in the past twenty years. Between these two the world faces a momentous choice. Thus far, political leaders are consistently opting for the ideology of growth. Indeed, they did so in the 1980s with greater consistency than ever before. Even though they have made occasional concessions to the demands of those who are committed to sustainability, this has little effect on their basic policies. The Clinton administration has demonstrated much greater environmental sensitivity, but the goal of growth remains primary.

Nevertheless, the number, confidence, and passion of those who are truly devoted to sustainability is increasing. They are not appeased by the sympathetic rhetoric they occasionally hear from those in high places, nor by the small steps taken from time to time for the sake of sustainability. They know, as many of those committed to growth do not, that the choice is fundamental.

It is important for those of us committed to sustainability to understand the power of the great god "growth" to control the hearts as well as the behavior of so many thoughtful people. Of course, some people adopt a religious position out of self-interest, and devotion to growth lends itself especially well to this use. But I am focusing on those whose conviction is sincere. Let us review the history of salvation that shapes their perception of the past, the present, and the future.

Most human beings throughout recorded history have lived near the threshold of survival. When the weather has been unfavorable, the soil has been depleted, or social discord disrupts normal patterns, hundreds of thousands have perished. Even when matters have gone well, the great majority have barely subsisted. The total production of goods has sufficed to make a few wealthy, but it has not sufficed to provide the amenities of life to the vast majority.

The industrial revolution changed this. It was, in part, a new organization of labor that enabled the same number of people, working the same amount of time, to produce far more goods. It was also a technological advance that harnessed fossil fuels in such a way as still further to increase the productivity of human labor. By these means, the economy grew.

The economists who observed this growth saw a major problem accompanying it. As economic growth led to increased income of workers, more of their children would survive, and the number of workers competing for jobs would increase. As a result, wages would fall back to subsistence levels. This meant that population growth would prevent the majority of people from improving their standard of living.

In fact, however, economic growth solved this problem as well. Through specializing in production and harnessing the energy in fossil fuels, the economy grew faster than the population, wages rose beyond mere subsistence, and prosperity led to less desire for large families. Family size dropped in industrialized nations, population growth slowed, and economic growth translated into a higher standard of living for the great majority. For the first time in human history, many of the poor came to enjoy what had previously been considered the luxuries of the rich, as well as many luxuries of which even the rich had not earlier dreamed.

This growth, which solved so many problems, was not to be taken for granted. There were many ways in which it could be inhibited or stopped. Under the best of circumstances it was erratic, being interrupted by periods of stagnation or decline. Economics became a science studying how growth could be maximized and its disruptions minimized. Neoclassical economics became the theology of those who saw economic growth as the savior of humankind from destitution, drudgery, and misery.

After World War II the religion of growth became global. Seeing the success of this religion in the developed countries, those that were not yet industrialized looked to it as their salvation as well. Global economic growth became the goal of international organizations as well as of national governments. The question was only to which sect to subscribe in pursuit of this growth. The World Council of Churches did not oppose growth when it committed itself to justice and participation. It only argued that these values should not be obscured or subordinated in the process of seeking growth.

No one can question that a great deal of suffering accompanied industrialization, especially in England, which pioneered it. No one can question that since World War II enormous suffering has been endured in many newly industrializing countries for the sake of the economic growth generated by industry. In many instances the sufferers could be controlled only by military governments.

In addition, industrialization, with its accompanying urbanization, intensifies social problems. Families are less stable. There is more loneliness and loss of meaning, accompanied by more use of alcohol and other drugs. Crime increases. Employment becomes less regular and secure.

Believers in growth acknowledge these social costs, but they are not deeply troubled by them. Some of them, they think, are outgrown as industrialization progresses. Wages rise, working conditions improve, and the unrest of labor declines. Democratic institutions guaranteeing civil rights replace authoritarian regimes.

Although urbanization increases some social problems, it also offers many advantages when compared with rural life. Further, affluence allows cities to respond to these social problems with social services. Indeed, for believers in growth, the presence of these problems only accents the need for the growth that allows societies to pay for the institutions required to deal with them.

These answers by devotees of growth have been convincing to most people. Accordingly, there have been few critics of the goal of growth until quite recently. Sustained criticism arose only in the sixties. It has increased rapidly since then, but it is still peripheral to the dominant discussion.

Criticism of growth arose with the discovery that growth beyond a certain point is destructive of the earth. We are already using resources much faster than they can be replenished. We are producing wastes much faster than nature's sinks can process them. The growth economy *will* end. The only questions are when its end will come, and whether humanity will be able to survive its demise.

For those who see this, it is overwhelmingly evident that our goal should not be economic growth but the development of an adequate economy that can be sustained indefinitely. That is a fundamentally different commitment. There is as yet no well-defined group working out what is involved in a sustainable society in the way that the economic profession has worked out what makes for growth.

Yet there are hundreds of groups and thousands of individuals who are thinking about these matters from a great variety of perspectives.

Those who are devoted to economic growth as the salvation of the world have not accepted the premise that the continuation of such growth is impossible. The orthodox reply is that resources are not limited for practical purposes. Of course, no one denies that particular resources are, in some absolute sense, limited, but human beings are nowhere close to these ultimate physical limits. When the economy does approach such limits, technology can develop new materials or energy sources to take the place of those that are exhausted.

Therefore, from the point of view of mainstream economic thinking, the need is to have sufficient capital to advance technology rapidly enough to avoid serious shortages. Since the accumulation of capital is a function of economic growth, the limits of particular resources reinforces the importance of economic growth. The widely drawn conclusion is that with sufficient economic growth, all the problems of the environment can be solved. Without it, they will not be solvable. While this orthodox doctrine is unconvincing to those who see the finitude and fragility of the earth system, at present it governs the affairs of the world.

When we speak of exhausting some resource, such as copper, we do not mean that there would in fact be no copper left in the planet. We mean that relative to a given technology, the remaining copper is not accessible for use. As technology advances, more copper will be available. The problem is cost. But when the cost of copper rises, more expensive technologies become cost-effective. Also there is greater incentive to find or create substitutes for copper in many of its various uses. From these facts most economists conclude that, in a free market, technology solves the problem of resource shortages.

The orthodox view that the problem is "cost," while accurate, usually obscures much of the cost. Economists take into account the costs to the companies engaged in extracting copper, but they rarely consider the environmental costs of larger and larger mining operations that are increasingly disruptive of the earth's surface. Also, because the exploitation of poorer and poorer resources requires more and more energy, the depletion of energy should be counted as a cost, but it rarely is. It is counted only at its market price. Fortunately, even within economic theory, there is an acknowledged, though usually neglected, basis for paying attention to these matters. Costs borne by those not directly engaged in the market transaction are called "externalities." It is recognized in principle, although rarely emphasized in practice, that these environmental costs as well as social ones should be internalized and included in the market price. This would steer growth in more benign directions.

This brings us to the problem of the costs of disposing of wastes. Here the orthodox commitment to growth confronts its greatest difficulties. It is hard to see how advances in technology can add to the capacity of the earth to cope with the greenhouse gases, for example. Of course, some reduction in these gases can be effected by technological advances in industry and transportation. But it is interesting that the most traditional economists advocate that we cope with the problems caused by global warming as they arise. When one properly discounts costs to be incurred twenty or thirty years from now, some argue, it is more economical to relocate people from flooded coastal areas then, or to build dikes to protect them, than to make the drastic changes needed to slow global warming.

These examples show that the religion of growth does not collapse when critics assert the unsustainability of the society to which it leads. The response is a denial of the charge. Its adherents believe that the problems can be resolved by the practices advocated by their theories. A religion rarely gives way before simple argumentation or even before evidence that outsiders see as disconfirming. To those of us who care deeply for the earth and its future, the proposal to continue to abuse it, and then use our technology to protect ourselves from the consequences of this abuse, is revolting. But to those who worship at the altars of economic growth, it appears quite sane and sensible. Indeed, it is highly attractive, since it enables them to go about the business to which they are accustomed and to which their skills are applicable.

On the other hand, even in the confrontation of one religion with another, argument has a role to play. To be effective, an argument cannot make assumptions rejected in the religion that is criticized. It must enter into the viewpoint that is criticized and show its failures in its own terms. I will offer an example of such an argument.

Even if production, that is, the gross national product (GNP), could continue to increase indefinitely in each country, much of this production must be recognized as "defensive." That is, GNP includes costs entailed by its increase, such as the costs of urbanization and protection from criminal activity. Increasingly, there are costs for environmental protection as well. If all the growth of the GNP were in these defensive costs, or if these defensive costs grew more rapidly than the GNP as a whole, then continued devotion to growth as measured by the GNP would have to be acknowledged as absurd. If a nation spent hundreds of billions of dollars relocating its people away from coastal lands and building dikes to protect those who remained, this would all be counted as increasing the GNP. In this sense, continued growth of the GNP might be sustained. But since this would not enable people to obtain more of the goods they desired, it would be absurd to claim that this kind of growth is beneficial.

The United States is already at the point where the costs of growth, even in strictly economic terms, exceed its benefits. Together with Clifford W. Cobb, I have tried to show this in an index of sustainable economic welfare (ISEW).[1] According to our figures, during the decade from 1980 through 1989, while per capita GNP grew by 20 percent, per capita sustainable economic welfare fell by 5 percent. In the next year, the last for which we have figures, per capita GNP fell slightly while per capita ISEW rose about 1 percent.

At least for me, this reduces to absurdity the arguments of those who want economic growth as measured by the GNP to go on indefinitely. The worship of growth began during a period in which this growth did seem to improve the lot of most people in those countries in which it occurred. The religion had a measure of justification. Continuing this devotion now, however, when the growth it pursues worsens the human condition, removes it from the status of a religion that should be taken seriously to that of sheer superstition. Nevertheless, we dare not minimize the power of this superstition to shape the thinking of intelligent and idealistic persons.

Now that we see that the growth to which the world has committed itself does not directly improve the human lot, we can raise other questions about the standard history of salvation, which I recited above in explaining the power of this religion. Was the life of the English yeomanry, before they were dispossessed by the enclosure movement, really as miserable and precarious as depicted? Was life in the cities of the Renaissance, with their guild economies, so terrible? Indeed, was the poverty of those days worse than the poverty of the present? Has economic growth benefited the poor?

We can also ask to what extent the prosperity of Europe and North America was generated through exploitation of

Latin America, Africa, and Asia, rather than by the efficiency of the manufacturing system. Certainly it was closely accompanied by the colonialism that destroyed indigenous cultures and exploited both natural and human resources throughout much of the world. Could it have occurred without this? Does it occur now apart from neocolonial exploitation of the tropical world?

If great claims are to be made for past achievements of the industrial system and its accompanying ideology of growth, they should be justified by comparisons of the total global situation before and after industrialization. Were human beings as a whole better off in the mid-nineteenth century than in the seventeenth? Are they better off today? The claim that industrialization has improved the human condition, even in strictly economic terms, is difficult to sustain. The issue today is whether, when unfettered from government regulations and social constraints, it can do so.

The global campaign for free trade expresses the faith that it can. From the point of view of those who reject the religion of growth, the amount of free trade we now have is doing appalling harm. The further extension through the North American Free Trade Agreement (NAFTA) and that proposed through the Uruguay round of the General Agreement on Tariffs and Trade (GATT) speed up the process of concentrating wealth in a few hands and degrading the global environment.

The growth establishment, finally realizing the importance of sustainability, has called for "sustainable development." By this it means "sustainable growth." This is made very clear in the *Brundtland Report*, which is the channel through which this phrase has passed into wide use. This report, as discussed in chapter 2, rightly recognizes the acute poverty widespread in much of the Third World, together with rapid population growth there, and calls for a five- to tenfold increase of production in the poorer nations.

The need for more goods and services in many parts of

the world is indisputable, and we can only be sympathetic toward this program. However, the report assumes the orthodox view that the poorer nations can grow only through trading with the richer ones. From this it follows that the First World must also increase its production and consumption manyfold. On a planet in which economic activity is already causing severe stresses in the natural environment, the call for a vast increase in this activity, whatever the rhetoric about sustainability, is absurd. Even if we followed all the wise recommendations of the *Brundtland Report* for more efficient use of resources, "sustainable growth" would remain an oxymoron.

What if the phrase *sustainable development* were taken away from those who are devoted to growth and employed by those who are committed to sustainability? Could we fill it with meaning? If not, are we not turning our backs on the teeming populations of Latin America, Africa, and southern Asia, condemning them to misery and worse?

The answer depends on what we can make of the other word in the title of this chapter: *community*. Alongside the dominant meaning of development as growth of per capita production and consumption, there is another meaning to be found in the term *community development*, and I believe sustainable community development *is* possible.

These two types of development are emphatically not complementary; indeed, they are antithetical. The dominant model of development as growth requires a systematic assault on existing communities as well as the rationalization of the values by which people in the tropical world have traditionally lived. Development there involves persuading individuals to subordinate their concern for their communities to their efforts to gain more goods for themselves. People who are content with meeting their basic needs must be taught to have insatiable wants. Those who have prized spiritual values above material ones must be persuaded to put material goods first. When persuasion and indoctrination do not suffice, economic and political force must be used.

This assault on community is not incidental to the industrial economy and to the economic theory associated with it. It is of its essence. In *The Great Transformation*, Karl Polanyi showed how in modernity, for the first time, instead of the economy being in the service of the society, the society was subordinated to the economy.[2] In modern economic theory, human relationships count for nothing. The *only* goal is increased production and consumption.

Community development reverses this great reversal and returns to the traditional view that the economy should be in the service of the community and that the values of the community govern what is considered to be development. It means that the process of development strengthens the community as community. While this formal statement has important meaning over against dominant images of development as growth, its material import is still indeterminate. There will be great variety with respect to what communities want.

This formal statement also requires an explanation of what is meant by "community." Herman Daly and I undertook some definition of it in *For the Common Good*,[3] but I will not try to summarize that here. I will, instead, use examples of communities and comment on what community development can mean in these instances.

In much of the tropical world, a large part of the population still lives in rural villages. Much of the practical outcome of adopting the principles of community development would be realized in and for these villages. This was the form of development advocated by Gandhi. A symbol of community development for him was the sewing machine. Technology of this sort would enable village women to become more productive. Similarly, an improved plough might help in the farming. The English economist E. F.

Schumacher called this kind of equipment "appropriate technology"[4] because it enables people to accomplish their tasks more successfully without changing the basic structure of their lives or their communal values, and it can be maintained and repaired by village people.

Of course, the desires of people in many villages will not be for sewing machines and better ploughs. In many places the most urgent problem is the lack of fuel for cooking. The greatest help may be to introduce solar cookers or stoves that can produce more heat with less wood or dung. Reforestation of local hillsides may be called for. In other places the major problems arise from the fact that development of the standard variety has made people dependent on fossil fuels and tractors that have become unaffordable and cannot be maintained. The need may be to return to a system based on the water buffalo.

In many places the problems of the villagers are caused by economic and political forces external to the villages. For example, they may be displaced to give the best land to agribusiness for production of export crops. Their need then is political organization against their oppressors and more generally a shift of public thinking from the present growth-oriented, export-driven development to the community development for which I am calling.

Community development enables villages to become more self-reliant instead of making them more dependent on decisions made about them by others. This requires that in essential matters they be able to survive on their own resources. Of course, this does not preclude trade. The village produces a surplus that it can exchange for goods it does not produce. But the less its survival depends on this exchange, the freer it is to seek fair terms of exchange and, thus, to escape the economic exploitation to which so many villages have been so long subjected. Community development moves toward self-sufficiency in essentials.

This kind of development does take place, especially in development programs sponsored by churches and other nongovernmental organizations. A fine example is World Neighbors, which, from its headquarters in Oklahoma City, has been supporting community development since 1951. The Asian Rural Institute in Nishinasuno, Japan, is another fine example. Even more important are the grassroots movements that have arisen independently throughout the less-affluent parts of the world.[5] The most important contribution of these movements is to gain some power for the poor so that their voices can no longer be ignored.

Even development of this kind sometimes increases the use of scarce materials, but it is more often a matter of developing more sustainable practices and more efficient use of renewable resources. If international development since World War II had followed the Gandhian model of community development, instead of adopting governmental policies aimed at overall economic growth, hundreds of millions of poor people would be better off, even though their standard of living as measured by per capita GNP would still be low.

Still, the shift from overall growth through industrialization to village development based on the felt needs of the villagers or generated by the people themselves is not a panacea. There are many patterns of injustice and cruelty that are entrenched in village life and traditional cultures. In particular, the treatment of women is often appalling. We are faced with the difficult decision of when and how to try to change the values of the people for whose welfare we are concerned without undercutting their ability to make decisions about their own lives.

Even if we decide against imposing our views of justice, there remain problems we cannot avoid. The felt needs of villagers can call for practices that have unsustainable consequences, whereas we must be committed to sustainable development. The problem is especially acute with regard to population growth. When villagers are consulted about their desires, they generally rank health and long life very high. They want the benefits of modern medicine. They also want large families. The result is continued population growth and the necessity that many of the children leave the village. The unsustainable growth of Third World cities may be slowed by improved life in the villages, but it will continue as long as villagers have more children than the village economy can assimilate.

I know of no easy solution to this problem. Indeed, it may be unsolvable, in which case much of the tropical world cannot avoid a holocaust. But, despite all ambiguities, there are two principles that those who seek to help with community development should affirm. First, the desire for children is increased by the need for old-age security. If there is another reliable way of caring for the old, some reduction of population growth can be anticipated. Second, women, especially when they can have roles in society outside the family, prefer to have fewer children. To empower women both to have more choices in life and to have a larger say in determining how many children to bear will reduce family size.

Following procedures such as these, the state of Kerala in India has greatly slowed its population growth in comparison with the rest of India. Its per capita income is about average for India, but human well-being as measured by infant mortality, life expectancy, and literacy is far higher. Thus, decline in population growth is only one of the gains that can be made through community development independently of economic growth.

In many cultures some of the needed changes will be resisted because of traditional values. Even with outside pressure, it may be impossible to effect them on a sufficient scale to make much difference. Furthermore, they may not suffice. But they are of such importance that they should have the highest priority in community development policies. A demographic transition of the sort that occurred without planning in Europe will not take place in most of the tropical world. Unless population growth is drastically curtailed by changes in social and governmental policies, there can be no attractive future. The alternative to lower birthrates will be higher deathrates caused by famine and disease.

Population growth is not the only problem of sustainability that a shift to community development may fail to solve. Others arise from the "tragedy of the commons," so well explained by Garrett Hardin some years ago.[6] Examples are numerous. An upstream community can solve its problems by dumping wastes into a river beyond the river's capacity to process them. Downstream communities must then deal with problems unfairly imposed upon them. An industrial community can avoid local pollution by building taller smokestacks, while the results in acid rain can devastate other communities far away. Fishing communities can "develop" by using more modern equipment to take a larger catch. But what profits each severally also destroys the fishery for all. Wiping out local elephants or baboons may make life easier in some communities, but it causes the extinction of species to the loss of the whole earth.

In these respects, also, community development, even for the sake of local communities, cannot simply be helping those communities to realize their *felt* needs. Restrictions must be observed. Ideally these restrictions are not simply imposed by alien authorities, but are agreed upon in a participatory way by communities of communities and communities of communities of communities reaching up to the United Nations. The restrictions will work, finally, only if the religion of sustainability, or what I have called *earth-ism*, becomes part of the fabric of life and faith in all of the communities.

In discussing sustainable development as community development I have focused on rural communities. Here the contrast with orthodox growth-oriented development is clearest. The latter sees traditional rural communities as in-efficient producers of agricultural goods to be replaced by agribusiness. This releases rural labor for industrial work in urban centers. In this orthodox scenario, this industry is the real engine of progress.

Community development, at least in much of the world, sees the most important matter as strengthening agricul-tural communities. However, if it is to provide an adequate model today, it must concern itself also with cities. By stop-ping, or at least slowing, the flow of population from the countryside to the cities, rural community development provides a contribution to dealing with urban problems. But while this contribution is necessary, it is far from suf-ficient. A new approach to urban development is also required.

Community development in urban areas becomes neigh-borhood development. Some neighborhoods already have some of the same cohesion as rural villages. Those con-cerned with development can then work with existing neighborhoods, discover felt needs, and respond to them. Neighborhoods can be strengthened politically and can become more nearly self-sufficient economically—even in the production of food! Where there is little neighborhood consciousness, the task of empowering them is more diffi-cult, but not impossible. Human beings have a natural ten-dency to identify with neighbors and with the sections of town in which they live.

In considering communities thus far, I have empha-sized small ones—rural villages and urban neighborhoods. Larger groupings of people, I have suggested, should be thought of as communities of communities. This would be true of cities, at least of large ones. In dealing with traditional villages, I did not go on to discuss these communities of communities, except for dealing with larger problems, for the villages can function quite separately. But even if urban neighborhoods recover some of the autonomy they have lost, they remain ineluctably parts of cities. It is of great importance that cities become communities of neighborhoods.

Cities as they are now built are inherently unsustainable. They require enormous input of energy for their very survival. They grow like cancers, often over the most fertile parts of the land, and claim resources from distant places. We have learned from William E. Rees and his associates at the University of British Columbia that the "appropriated carrying capacity" or "ecological footprint" of a city can be measured as the sum of various areas external to the city whose produce the city requires for its functioning.[7] A city can only be thought of as sustainable together with the regions required to supply it with goods. At present we have no models of sustainable cities.

The most positive proposal of which I am aware is that of Paolo Soleri.[8] His arcologies would meet their energy requirements chiefly from passive solar power and would eliminate the need for motor transportation within the city. They would occupy far less land and would produce most of their needed agricultural products nearby. Together with the surrounding countryside, they could become largely autonomous economic units. Further, they would encourage the kind of participation by their citizens that makes for true community.

The United States is perhaps the most difficult country in which to implement the vision of relatively self-sufficient communities. Americans have worshipped the great god "growth" so long both in theory and in practice that stable communities, either rural or urban, have become rare. Even those of us who recognize the need for community prize our mobility. We may find it exciting to experiment with community living, but few of us want to make long-term commitments. In our resulting loneliness, we know how important relationships are, but we have internalized the values of individualism too deeply to set them aside.

Precisely for this reason, this is the country in which experimentation in such communities is most widespread, most important, and most fruitful. To use a now overused term, we are looking for "postmodern" communities. We have so embodied the values and ideologies of the modern world that traditional communities are too broken to inhibit us or restrict our vision. We are truly free to experiment.

In much of the world, the task of concerned people is to strengthen communities against the onslaught of policies aimed at economic growth and to help them find directions of development that fulfil their hopes without damage to others. But here in this country, our task is to re-invent community in a way that from the outset is inspired by a global vision. Some of what we learn in our experiments may be useful in parts of the world where traditional community still lives. Some of it may also be useful in the vast urban slums of developing countries. But whether or not it is useful elsewhere, it is imperative, for the sake of all, that our own nation re-invent itself. That re-invention will have to be from the bottom up in terms of communities, not individuals.

At the same time that we work from below, we must be aware that we are always vulnerable to changes from above. While we seek to create an economy that does not depend on capital controlled by remote financiers, we must be aware that if we become threats to those financiers, they have political and economic power at their disposal sufficient to destroy us. The courts to which not long ago we could turn to check this power have now become its instruments. We can see how this works in the case of the Christic Institute which for some years was able to bring the power of the law to bear on corporate and even governmental criminals. Eventually it undertook to expose the complicity of the truly powerful in vast networks of international crime, only to be wiped out financially by court decisions that made it impossible for it to present the damaging evidence it had amassed against high officials. Postmodern communities will be tolerated as long as they are an aberration harmless to the great centers of financial and political power. But once their revolutionary significance becomes clear, their ability to survive will be truly tested.

The social costs of growth will continue to become more apparent: lower wages, reduced environmental protection, deteriorating education, increased crime and drug abuse, growing violence, intensifying hatred of those who are different. But we should not assume that these changes will lead to abandonment of the religion of growth. On the contrary, we will be told that all these problems can be solved only by economic growth. As now, so also in the future, the people as a whole may well be persuaded. And as long as they are persuaded, the new communities we need will appear as an interesting fringe activity, a luxury that few can afford.

This is not the only possible scenario. The fact is that our economic and human deterioration is a result of policies adopted for the sake of growth. This ironic truth can be voiced in a way that may enable millions of people to realize that the emperor has no clothes, that economism has failed them, and that the god for whom they have been asked to sacrifice is in truth only an idol. And if *that* happens, then the very different religion of sustainability or earthism will appear as the evidently true one, and new economic thinking, ordered to sustainability, will arise. If *that* happens, then the urgency of developing new communities will become apparent.

As an afterword, I would like to comment on the term *sustainable*. It has played a very positive role and can continue to do so as it expresses the way more and more people are already thinking. This is a practical and politically important reason for its continued use.

However, like all words and the ideas they bring to life, it has limitations. The focus on sustainable human communities remains thoroughly anthropocentric. It makes us aware of the important fact that many of the abuses we inflict on the ecosystem are unsustainable and that we will ourselves suffer from their consequences. But it is time to go beyond this anthropocentrism to think in biocentric or geocentric ways.

My own view is that grounding these, and ultimately more adequate than either, is authentic theocentric thinking. The World Council of Churches, in calling on its members to consider the "integrity of creation," has moved in this direction.[9] Communities should not only be sustainable, but also should allow other species to live in a healthy way and should leave space for wilderness.

In the end, indeed, I doubt that people will be motivated to take the actions needed for their own survival if they are not concerned for other creatures as well. Individuals who systematically seek their private self-interest do not attain the relations with others that they really need and want. Nations rarely behave in their true long-term enlightened self-interest if their people are not motivated by wider concerns. A humanity concerned only for its own survival will inevitably take too narrow a view of what is required to assure that survival. Only as the object of our devotion is extended to the whole earth will we act in ways that will assure our own continued participation in a healthy biosphere. That is why I have introduced into this chapter, from time to time, the term *earthism*, which was explained in the previous chapter. Earthism calls not merely for sustainable human communities but for human communities committed to the sustenance of the wider ecological communities of which they are a part.

4

To Pay or
Not to Pay?

The debt crisis, the threat to our nation's financial system, has been an important concern since the early 1980s. If a number of the major debtor nations of the less-industrialized world abruptly ceased paying interest on their debts to U.S. and European banks, some of the largest of these banks might become insolvent. The banking system is so interconnected that a few such failures would have extensive repercussions and could lead to financial chaos. A crisis of this sort would wreak havoc in the lives of many people and whole countries. Much that we have come to take for granted would be endangered.

On the other hand, by now, the danger of such drastic disruption is largely past. Abrupt cancellation of debt by several debtors would still create major problems, but steps have been taken to reduce these to manageable proportions. Banks have written off part of their debts and built up reserves. Governments are prepared to step in where necessary. In short, the operations of the international financial community since 1980 have dealt successfully with this major threat to the global banking system. One of its great historic successes is that it rose to the challenge of the crisis and saved the system.

From the perspective of the governments of debtor nations, also, the problem has eased. They have reorganized their economies in such a way that the debts can be paid. In many cases debt payments are not as large a portion of gross national product (GNP) as once was the case.

Viewed from the side of the poor in the debtor nations, however, the problem grows worse year by year. From this perspective it is not so much a crisis as a chronic disease for which no cure is in sight. The disease is made systematically worse by the policies that have successfully ended the crisis. Accordingly, the remainder of this chapter views the international financial situation chiefly from the perspective of the Third World.

Historical perspective will help explain what is now taking place in most of the world. The present global financial system came into being in 1945 at Bretton Woods. The Western victors of World War II there created three great institutions, which continue to exist and play a dominant role in the system; their function was to ensure rising prosperity around the world. This would be achieved by increased worldwide trade, for which the smooth functioning of global finance is required.

The first of these institutions, the General Agreement on Tariffs and Trade (GATT), encourages the increase of trade by a gradual and orderly reduction of trade barriers. GATT also provides ways of adjudicating disputes that arise among nations and has the economic power to enforce its decisions.

The second institution is the International Monetary Fund (IMF). Its function is to deal with temporary fiscal problems that arise when currencies are seriously out of line or nations have problems in meeting their international responsibilities. The IMF took the lead in resolving the debt crisis of the early eighties.

The International Bank for Reconstruction and Development, usually known more simply as the World Bank, is the third institution. The World Bank makes long-term loans to developing countries to fund projects that will advance their economies.

For at least twenty-five years this post–World War II world order accomplished its goals. During the fifties and sixties the global economy grew fairly steadily at 5 percent or more a year. Indeed, in twenty-five years it tripled in size. Of course, there was borrowing during that period, but debt was not a major problem. Much of the borrowed money, which mostly came from governments or the World Bank, was invested in ways that contributed to growth. It was often used partly to fund development programs that were supported also by outright grants. In any case, interest on most of these loans was quite low, sometimes less than inflation, so that even loans included an element of gift.

Looking back, we can see that the situation was not entirely positive. Indeed, even at the time many of us had major concerns about what was transpiring. Yet prior to 1970 the great majority of idealistic Christians supported the basic direction of the global economy and the institutions that made it possible. We were committed to economic development of Third World countries, and our major criticisms were that more money should be flowing in gifts, loans, and investments to them.

Any serious political concerns were often thought of as separate from the economic ones. Many Third World countries were ruled by authoritarian regimes that allowed very little freedom of expression on the part of the people and often treated dissenters brutally, but we were not aware that the policies adopted for economic growth made such regimes necessary. These policies required the shift of agriculture from subsistence farming to agribusiness, meaning that force often had to be used to remove peasants from their land. In order for the products to compete on the world market, industrial development entailed very low wages and hard working conditions. Labor, therefore, could not be allowed to organize to protest conditions and demand a larger share of the profits.

Prior to the seventies few of us noticed the rapid exploitation of nonrenewable resources and the deterioration of the natural environment that were involved in economic development. These were additional costs borne by the poor. Today we realize that they have global consequences.

We were aware then, and are even more keenly aware now, that the economic growth was unevenly distributed. A few nations, such as South Korea, Taiwan, Hong Kong, and Singapore grew rapidly into impressive prosperity. On the other hand, economic growth in many countries in Latin America and, especially, in Africa barely kept pace with the increase of population.

Whatever the problems connected with global development from 1945 to 1970, most Christians saw them as temporary delays on the way to realizing the shared dream of global prosperity. The economic success of a few Third World countries encouraged the expectation that in time all would follow in their path. There was reasonable hope that authoritarian governments would give way to democratic ones. There was little complacency, but the great majority of us assumed that the world was making genuine progress and that eventually poverty of the most degrading sort would be ended.

In the seventies the system did not work as well. The first problem had to do with the U.S. dollar, on which the whole global system was based. By 1970, it could no longer bear this weight, and readjustments were required.

More important were the problems engendered by the Organization of Petroleum Exporting Countries (OPEC). In the early seventies OPEC succeeded in raising the price of oil drastically and abruptly. The resulting "oil shock" had a significant effect on First World countries, but its greatest impact was in the Third World. Much development there had involved a shift from labor-intensive to energy-intensive modes of production. This was involved, for example, in the Green Revolution, which introduced far more productive strains of grain, but ones that required a shift from primary reliance on solar energy and manure to heavy use of petroleum products. When the cost of this energy tripled overnight, the economic hardship in some countries was acute.

In the long run it turned out that the windfall of cash to the OPEC countries was even more disruptive than the immediate problem for Third World countries of paying for oil. The oil-producing states accumulated many billions of dollars for which they had no immediate use. They deposited this money in First World banks, which then, of course, needed to find borrowers.

To understand the magnitude of the sums available to lend, it is necessary to recall our federal reserve system. A bank that receives a billion dollars from outside the U.S. banking system can deposit this with the government. It can then lend about ten billion dollars to its customers. There was insufficient demand in the First World to absorb these funds. Hence the banks sent representatives throughout the Third World to persuade potential borrowers to borrow. These representatives were rewarded in proportion to the amount of money they were successful in lending, not in terms of the economic wisdom of the loans.

The banks were not particularly interested in how the money was spent. They were, however, interested in the security of their loans. This meant that they preferred to lend to governments or to companies that could arrange for gov-

ernment guarantee of repayment. Since Third World business was often closely tied to government, this was usually
possible.

The result of this policy on the part of commercial banks
was a vast increase in Third World debt. Between 1973 and
1983 it rose sixfold, from 150 billion dollars to 900 billion
dollars. Most of the increased indebtedness was to commercial banks. When certain governments, such as Mexico,
began showing signs of inability to pay around 1980, commercial bank lending to Third World countries declined
drastically and the rate of increase of debt slowed dramatically. Nevertheless, ten years later the total debt has increased another 400 billion dollars to 1.3 trillion dollars.

We can easily understand why banks wanted to lend
their money. But we must reflect also on why Third World
countries agreed to borrow. Should they not have been able
to foresee the problems this would cause them in the future?

First, there are, of course, legitimate reasons for borrowing. Some loans benefit, rather than burden, the future. The
availability of this money could, therefore, be viewed as a
great opportunity for speeding up economic development.
If a nation can invest one billion dollars in industries that
then make 10 percent profit, while it pays 6 percent interest
on its debt, it will retain 4 percent of this profit for further
investment. Especially since interest rates were low in relation to inflation, borrowing the offered money could seem a
prudent and wise policy. Let us assume that some portion
of the borrowed money went to such projects, and we can
applaud this. The problem is that most did not. Our list
continues with these other uses in view.

Second, a nation that is having difficulty paying for
needed imports, such as newly expensive oil, will certainly
be tempted by the ready availability of a loan to solve its
immediate problem. Unfortunately, this understandable

choice only postpones the problem until the future, when the loan must be repaid with interest, often with less available money.

Third, much money loaned to governments was invested in bureaucratically managed business. We now know more clearly than in 1970 that such business is rarely efficient. Many government businesses required tax support in order to survive. Hence they could not contribute to the repayment of the debt. Of course, not all privately operated investments succeeded either.

Fourth, in addition to financing imports essential for the economy, loans could be used to pay for luxury imports for the middle class. By "luxury" I mean in many instances goods that the middle class in the First World take for granted; so we should not be critical of the new middle classes of the Third World for demanding them. But these consumer purchases added nothing to the ability of the Third World to repay the debts.

Fifth, especially because many of the borrowers were governments run by the military, the borrowed funds supported larger and more modern military establishments. Again, these contributed nothing to the ability to repay.

Sixth, large sums were spent on what are often called prestige monuments. The most famous of these is a replica of St. Peter's Cathedral built in the jungles of West Africa. But many other buildings of no economic value have been built by authoritarian rulers.

Seventh, an astonishingly large part of the money loaned to Third World governments ended up in the First World bank accounts of the elites of those nations. This is called capital flight. These loans thus made a few people extremely rich but did nothing for their countries.

As long as interest rates remained low and more money could be easily borrowed, repayment was not a serious problem despite the misuse of so much of the original loans. However, interest on these loans did not remain low. It was tied to interest rates in the United States, and these soared at the end of the seventies. Interest payments that had been only a little above inflation rose to 10 percent above inflation! They suddenly became a major factor in the budgets of debtor nations, a factor that could not be dealt with apart from drastic changes of some sort. The inclination of several governments was to repudiate their debts as the only viable solution.

This was the debt crisis to which the IMF successfully responded. It worked with Mexico and other countries to develop a system by which payments on the debts could be made in an orderly way. This involved new loans from the IMF and other sources and the rescheduling of payments. But the price of this help was basic change, called structural adjustment by the IMF, in the economic system of the countries involved. It is important that we understand what is involved.

If Third World countries are to pay their debts, two conditions must be met. First, since debt must be repaid in dollars or other hard currencies, the country must achieve a favorable balance of international trade. That is, its exports must exceed its imports by a sufficient margin to earn the needed foreign currency. Second, governments must organize their finances so that income exceeds expense, other than debt payments, by an amount sufficient to allow such payment.

To gain a favorable balance of trade, a country typically devalues its currency, making imports more expensive and exports more competitive. This is effective only if costs, especially labor, within the country are held at the earlier level as measured in the now-devalued currency, which is accomplished by freezing wages. By this method, the wage of Mexican workers, measured in U.S. dollars, was cut to less than half of what it had been before "adjustment." These low wages make Mexican products cheap on the international market and attract capital investment from outside.

The other method of gaining hard currency is by speeding up exports of whatever commodities are available. In Third World countries, these are usually raw materials. For example, rapid cutting of forests is characteristic of the export-driven strategy imposed by the IMF. Actually, in a number of debtor countries the major source of hard currency for repayment of debts comes from the sale of illegal drugs. One reason it is so difficult to reduce the production of drugs in Third World countries is that the national economies in many of them are now dependent on this export.

To improve the national budget, IMF recommends the privatization of government corporations. The sale of these businesses realizes money for the government, and private ownership is likely to lead to greater efficiency in their operation. The IMF also requires major reductions in governmental expenditures, which, in principle, could be in the military budget, but, in practice, are almost always in social services. Hence a drastic reduction in services combined with lower wages typically characterizes structural readjustment. Finally, in its commitment to the idea that free trade promotes the economic growth of all, the IMF also urges reduction of barriers to trade and to foreign investments. It does this in part to force indigenous business to become more efficient so as to compete with foreign business.

One method of actually reducing the debt, rather than simply servicing it, is debt for equity exchange. A bank may reduce the debt in exchange for acquiring property or businesses in the debtor country. For example, when a government is selling off its holdings, it may give some of these to a creditor in exchange for debt reduction.

This combination of policies has enabled the great majority of debtors to reduce or continue to service their debts, and in this sense, has been a great success; the debt problem is no longer thought of as a crisis. Our international institutions have risen to the challenge and solved it. Especially with the decline of interest rates, debt payments have become a smaller portion of national income in most Third World countries, so that pressure on their governments to cease making payments has declined.

Nevertheless, as noted above, total debt has continued to increase. There has been a shift of some of this debt from commercial banks to governments and to international institutions. That is, new loans from public institutions have enabled debtors to make payments to private ones. This means that taxpayers in the First World, who provide the funds used by governments and intergovernmental institutions, have repaid some of the debt to the commercial banks. But this debt is still not significantly reduced.

The results of these policies have been favorable for the international financial community and the First World generally. After several decades following World War II in which capital flowed primarily from north to south, a reversal has come about. Susan George summarizes the new situation in this way.[1] According to the Organization for Economic Cooperation and Development, "between 1982 and 1990, total resource flow to developing countries amounted to $927 billion," much of it in loans that must be repaid with interest. During these years "developing countries remitted in debt service alone $1,345 billion (interest and principal) to the creditor countries." This involves a transfer of $418 billion in addition to uncalculated payments of "royalties, dividends, repatriated profits, underpaid raw materials, and the like."

The lower wages and reduced social services characteristic of structural adjustment indicate who pays. The poor are being further exploited in order to make these payments. Indeed, it would be hard to exaggerate the suffering imposed on the poor today in the Third World in order to maintain the global financial system. The appalling decline of health services and education in much of Africa is but one example. Of course, it can be blamed on other circumstances, but the siphoning off of government funds for debt payment is a major factor.

This whole system has negative consequences in the United States as well. The insistence that Third World countries all export more than they import means that some nation must import more than it exports. This role has been adopted chiefly by the United States, but at a high price. The United States now has by far the largest external debt of any country. Also, real wages for U.S. workers have fallen 17 percent in the past seventeen years, despite the fact that cheap imports have slowed inflation. The money that flows to First World coffers from the Third World poor does not improve the lot of ordinary people in the United States.

Considering the enormous suffering in the Third World required to continue to service debts that still grow in size, why do these debtor countries continue to pay? The question needs to be considered in light of the fact that historically it has not been unusual for governments to renege on their foreign debts, as most did during the Great Depression. Yet the suffering in many Third World countries today is worse than anything that occurred in Europe and North America during that depression.

One reason that these countries continue to pay is that the structural adjustment forced upon them does not distribute the pain equally. Most of the suffering is borne by those with the least political power. Those who make the political decisions continue to live well. Indeed, those who make the political decisions have much to lose by debt repudiation, which would drastically disrupt trade and put an end to new credits. Then it would be hard to obtain the imported energy and other goods needed to operate the factories and agribusiness that support the middle class. Since the economy as a whole has become tied to international trade, and since so much production is for export, the disruptions involved would be enormous. Also, the luxuries to which the middle class has become addicted would become unattainable.

Furthermore, we have seen that the elite has enormous wealth in First World banks and other investments. This would be subject to seizure to pay creditors, as would government assets abroad. In short, the cost to the Third World elite of failure to service the debt would be very great.

A different question that is sometimes raised is appropriate for Christians to ask: *Should* they pay? We can see that as long as the poor do the paying, the elite will want the debt servicing to continue. But do we as Christians favor continuation of this system?

Obviously, we who assert a preferential option for the poor cannot affirm the present system. It is a violation of all we believe. But can we propose something better? Should we, for example, advocate the forgiveness of all debts with our governments, that is, taxpayers, stepping in to prevent financial catastrophes in First World banks?

Perhaps, but we do need to recognize what is involved. As long as we treat nations as nations, then we must consider that these nations indebted themselves freely and are obligated to pay what they agreed to pay. Even when the present government differs from the one that borrowed the money, international law emphasizes that this does not affect their international responsibilities. Otherwise it would be impossible to develop lasting international agreements of any kind. Even revolutionary governments often assure the world community of their intention to honor international obligations. Simply releasing all debtors from their legally contracted obligations may make continuation of the whole global economic system very difficult.

On the other hand, when we see that those persons who borrowed the money and profited from it are not those who are in fact paying it back, we may conclude that the present situation is so vicious that it must be ended at all costs. In this respect a better ending would be refusal to pay on the part of debtor countries, since that would allow confiscation of the assets of the elite, most of which were gained by the borrowing. If, to avoid confiscation, these funds were repatriated, that would also be a gain. Such an eventuality would result in some cases if governments and international agencies ceased to aid the debtors in making their payments to the commercial banks. The cessation of such aid would also mean the end of transferring public funds to the commercial banks, and it would force these banks to share in the losses occasioned by their irresponsible lending policies.

Some of the most impoverished debtor countries, especially in Africa, may well be allowed to reduce their payments or even stop them completely without severe punishment. Commercial banks have sold some of these debts at large discounts and have already written off much of the rest. Several European countries have turned loans into gifts. The debts are small from the point of view of creditors, and the assets of these countries are often not attractive. They are not important actors in the world trade system. No significant disruption would occur from further debt forgiveness in some instances.

However, as long as the global system is committed to global economic growth, no policy that would disrupt international trade and financial institutions will be considered. Failure to make payments will not be tolerated on the part of any of the major debtors and trading partners. If the time comes when sufficient funds can no longer be extracted from the poor and by exploiting the natural environment, payments will be made by transferring ownership of property. This will go on as long as the elite prefer

such transfer to losing their own assets. The future prospects for most people in these countries are very bleak
indeed.

There is an alternative, but it would require a complete
reversal of national and international policy. Since Bretton
Woods, the world has been committed to economic growth
as the solution to all of its major problems. The alternative
would require us to acknowledge that economic growth
and the policies adopted to bring it about *are* the major
problems themselves.

Most Christians do not understand this. They still assume that failing to increase the size of the economy of a
Third World country would condemn its people to miserable poverty. Recognizing that the very policies adopted
for the sake of growth have reduced so many to miserable
poverty is a profound reversal of perspective, a kind of
metanoia. If the church can lead in this reversal it will per-
form an enormous service to the world's people as well as
to the global system of living things.

This alternative does not reject growth altogether. There
are kinds of growth that are truly needed in many places.
But this approach does not aim at growth as such. It aims at
meeting the needs of people in a sustainable way and improving the quality of their lives.

The Dag Hammarskjöld Foundation, established in 1975,
has proposed "another development."[2] This development
operates in terms of five principles: it will be (1) need oriented; (2) endogenous; (3) self-reliant; (4) ecologically sound;
and (5) based on structural transformation.

Focusing development on human need obviously seems
desirable. Those people who favor continuation of the
global growth policies now in effect certainly assert, and in
many cases believe, that these policies are designed to meet
human need. The question is whether they do so. Consider
the case of structural adjustment. Its intended effect is to

enable the country to service its debts. This requires reduced social spending, hence reduced governmental efforts to meet the needs of the poor, which is counter to the expressed goal. However, many economists will argue that in the long run keeping the global economy growing will meet more human needs than responding to human needs immediately here and now, when that would disrupt the institutions that support this growth.

In my opinion, on the other hand, the policies aimed at global growth as the means of benefiting the poor in fact make the rich richer and the poor poorer. They also cause environmental damage of a sort that affects everyone, rich and poor alike, through destruction of the ozone layer, global warming, and exhaustion of natural resources, leaving less for future generations. The planet cannot endure continuation of such growth.

"Another development" proposes that we work directly to meet human needs, formulating our policies for this purpose here and now, and making the availability of food, clothing, and shelter to all our priority. This is not to be done by shipping food from places where there is surplus production and making poor people in other countries dependent on such charity. On the contrary, the way people obtain food should be endogenous—culture- and location-specific—and promote self-reliance. Rather than destroying traditional cultures and communities, "another development" seeks to strengthen and use them. What is often called "community development" begins with villagers where they are and helps them to meet their felt needs better. It does so in a way that enables them to maintain control over their own lives rather than become dependent on imported technologies that can be serviced only by outsiders.

"Another development" aims to be ecologically sound. Today, we might speak of sustainability. To have a sustainable economy, a nation can use its renewable resources

only in ways that nature can replenish. Nonrenewable resources must be used at a pace that allows substitution of
renewable ones as the nonrenewable ones are depleted.

The fact that *sustainable development* is a term now accepted in the international community is the main source of
hope that alternatives to the dominant growth-oriented
paradigm may get some consideration in the near future.
Most of those who have accepted this term assume that it
means business almost as usual, with some attention to
specific environmental crises as they force themselves on
widespread human notice. But any serious reflection on the
term shows that continuation of the present growth-
oriented policies is unsustainable on a much more fundamental basis. When those who are now committed to these
policies argue that there are no alternatives that do not con-
sign much of the world to misery, it is important to have
well-articulated explanations available of "another development."

Finally, "another development" recognizes that traditional societies, like modern ones, have features that work
against justice and sustainability and the freedom of communities to shape their own lives. Many traditional structures keep the poor both poor and powerless. Exploitation
is not an invention of modernity. To work with the poor to
claim their rights is an essential part of "another development."

The Dag Hammarskjöld Foundation focuses on development of the economies of the Third World. However, the
principles it affirms are applicable in the industrialized
world as well. Indeed, if they are not applied in the industrialized world, it is unlikely that they will be adopted by
less-industrialized nations. And even if they were adopted
by the latter, the continued unsustainable practices of the
rich nations would doom the global system.

If the world economy made the U-turn from growth-
orientation to "another development," there would be more

options with respect to debt. Preoccupation with debt repayment is part and parcel of the growth system, of which increase in international trade is a cornerstone. A shift away from that system would relieve the pressure to ensure that all major debtors service their debts faithfully. The resulting difficulties in trade could prod countries around the world to become more self-reliant economically. Governments and intergovernmental agencies could step aside and leave settlement to negotiations between debtors and creditors. Where agreements are not reached and debtors fail to pay, assets of the elite of debtor nations could and should be seized as partial repayment. What cannot be collected from elites would no longer be wrung from the poor.

In a decentralizing world, the concentration of financial power in huge transnational banks would decline. If failure to collect on loans led to the failures of some major financial institutions, this would not necessarily be catastrophic. On the other hand, if governments decided that the disruption within their countries would be too great, they could intervene. But the solutions should not pass on to taxpayers all the losses sustained by banks because of irresponsible lending policies.

Generous-spirited Christians are likely to object that the reversal of direction I recommend would work against the great development projects sponsored by the World Bank and some First World governments. Many are still convinced that these projects are essential for any hope of prosperity in the less-industrialized nations. If the good society is understood to be, necessarily, very much like the present societies of North America, Europe, and Japan, then a case can be made in support of this view. But if these projects entail the suffering involved in earlier stages of capitalist economic development without the prospect of resulting prosperity, and if in the meantime they are environmentally destructive, then the decline of such projects need not be a reason to delay moving toward "another development."

A case study will help to clarify the issues. The largest project now being promoted by the World Bank, indeed, the largest river project ever planned, is the Narmada Valley Project in India. The World Bank views this as a showcase of its contributions to economic development. An excellent summary of the story of this project is found in Paul Ekins's *A New World Order: Grassroots Movements for Social Change.*[3]

In the view of the World Bank, the Narmada River "is one of [India's] least used—water utilization is currently about 4% and tons of water effectively are wasted every day when it could be put to use for the benefit of the region."[4] Plans are for two very large dams and twenty-eight others, together with three thousand smaller projects. The goal is to irrigate vast tracts of land, provide drinking water, promote pisciculture, produce electrical power, and control floods.

Of course, there are costs in addition to that of building these dams. The dams will submerge around twenty-five thousand acres, about half of which is forested. India's Department of Environment and Forests estimated the value of this land at four hundred billion rupees. If this figure were accepted, it would upset all the cost-benefit calculations used to support building the dams. Environmentalists also point out that siltation and evaporation, as well as salinization of irrigated lands and effects on downstream ecosystems, are not adequately considered in evaluating the positive contribution of the dams. In addition, the increase in diseases that follow from such constructions has been ignored.

The World Bank does recognize, to be sure, that about two hundred thousand people will have to be relocated. Its policy guidelines call for their favorable resettlement as part of the expense of the project. However, the implementation of the policy is another matter, as its own studies have shown. In fact, these people are condemned to miserable poverty and dependence. Recognizing this, they have become increasingly militant in their opposition to the project and are refusing to move.

None of these problems is reducing World Bank enthusiasm for the project. Human and environmental losses are minimized, and economic gains are emphasized. In these ways the World Bank carries forward a tradition of development through large-scale projects, especially dams.

Critics of the dam have proposed alternative ways of dealing with some of the real problems to which the dam project responds. For example, one student of the region "recommends a broad strategy including fuller utilization of existing installed irrigation capacity (58 per cent of this capacity in Gujarat and 70 per cent in M[adhya] P[radesh] is apparently unused), more economical use of water, especially by industry, and a strategy to improve ecological balance, through afforestation and agroforestry, improved dry farming technology, erosion control measures and small-scale water harvesting."[5] R. Engineer has shown that where some of these measures have been applied, the problem of water shortage has in fact been solved![6] Unfortunately, these inexpensive small-scale responses to problems do not appeal to those responsible for economic development. They do not make dramatic contributions to economic growth, although they produce far less human suffering and environmental damage and meet real human needs more effectively than the big projects do.

The basic thesis of this chapter is that there is no real solution to the chronic disease of indebtedness of Third World countries as long as they, and global leaders generally, are committed to economic growth. For the sake of growth, trade must be safeguarded and increased. That can only occur in the context of orderly international financial transactions. The Bretton Woods institutions have been brilliantly successful in maintaining this context.

Yet even within this context some minor improvements can be made. The IMF could pressure borrowers to do more of their budget cutting in the area of military expenditures. It could insist on heavier taxation of the rich and maintenance of minimum services for the poor, and it could bring some environmental considerations into play. Also, without major disruption of the system, some extremely impoverished nations could have their debts reduced or forgiven. These are countries that are more or less written out of the global trading system and are likely to be cut off to sink or swim on their own.

But these minor adjustments will not touch the main problem. Economic growth in the Third World has always been at the expense of the poor and the environment. This exploitation is simply exaggerated and accelerated by the need to pay back the money that was unwisely, or even corruptly, borrowed. Continuing the policies that aim at global economic growth will only intensify the suffering of the poor.

The other side of the thesis is that the energies of the world could be devoted to the strategy of "another development." In the context of a shift in this direction, most debts could be reduced, forgiven, or repudiated gradually without massive damage. Instead of continuing to exploit the powerless, such a strategy would undertake to empower them and allow them to use their labor to improve their own lot.

The assumption underlying all of this is that when Christians understand the real choices facing the world, they must opt for "another development." However difficult it may be to reverse direction on a global level, that must be our goal. We cannot willingly continue to participate in a global system that robs the poor to enrich the wealthy and degrades the planet that is left to future generations.

5
Against
Free Trade

The relation of trade and development has been dealt with tangentially in earlier chapters. It comes to focus in public debates about particular trade agreements such as the North American Free Trade Agreement and the Uruguay round of the General Agreement on Tariffs and Trade. This chapter treats the general issue of free trade with special reference to its effects on economic development in Mexico.

In *Mexico: Development Strategies for the Future*, Denis Goulet identifies neoliberal and nationalistic as the two basic options proposed for development. He explains them as follows:

> The neoliberal model favors (1) a high degree of centralization in decision making, thus perpetuating the extant mode; (2) elitist control over information, power, and resources accompanied by a ritualistic homage paid to the "masses" and their organizations; and (3) a cultural priority assigned to industry and to the industrialization of agriculture, with a strong orientation toward making Mexico competi-

tive (and a strong earner of foreign currencies) in global markets.

Conversely, a "nationalistic" strategy favors (1) greater decentralization at all levels—in government, the distribution of funds, the assignment of responsibility, and the diffusion of information; (2) widespread popular participation in decisions from below, in the case of formal organizations, and from outside the system, in the case of dealings with the government or the economic power structure (banks, government agencies, etc.) and (3) a high priority given to making small agricultural production (or ejidal cultivators, either singly or in collective organizations, family farmers, etc.) more productive thanks to a cluster of supports enabling it to compete financially and technically with larger commercial farms principally oriented to exports. The smaller farm sector will aim, at first, at satisfying the basic needs of those working in it and, later, at creating an expanding base for economic well-being.[1]

Mexico has continued down the first track with accelerating speed. This has been partly because of external pressure related to international debt and partly due to the doubtless sincere convictions of Mexico's economist president, Carlos Salinas. Restructuring is a fact of life and necessary for the sake of increasing Mexico's exports and its attractiveness to external investors. Policymakers hope that this will enable it to pay its debts, thus supporting the international economic system, and that, in the long run, Mexico will become a successful industrial society.

The cornerstone of this program is lowering trade barriers, especially with the United States, to attract capital to Mexico. If goods produced in Mexico can enter the United States with little or no tariff or delay, then U.S. companies can be encouraged to move their production of goods for the U.S. market across the border where wages and standards for workplace safety are much lower, and where the extra costs of production connected with safeguarding the environment are much less. The U.S.-owned factories, the *maquiladoras*, that have sprung up along the border to take advantage of this opportunity already employ half a million Mexican workers. As the North American Free Trade Agreement (NAFTA) goes into effect, the assumption is that many more such factories will be built. This is usually treated, of course, as a great success story: free trade brings jobs to Mexico; the country's gross national product (GNP) rises; and prices of goods in the United States are reduced.

But Mexico also pays a high price for that "success," or rather, the poor people in Mexico pay. Restructuring means lower wages and fewer social services for the poor. The minimum wage is now set at fifty-nine cents an hour, and the average wage in the maquiladoras is no more than a dollar an hour. Working conditions are sometimes shocking, with minimal protection of the health and safety of workers. Protesting workers are ignored, demoted, or fired. Nearby residential areas lack basic amenities. And the Rio Grande has been turned into a chemical sewer.

Goulet speaks not only of industry but also of the industrialization of agriculture. This, too, is proceeding and is closely tied to attracting U.S. investment and to exporting to the United States. The major obstacle here has been land reform programs of an earlier period designed to ensure that Mexican peasants keep their land. Peasants without capital have not been productive, and their products cannot compete with those of large estates. The nationalistic option Goulet outlines deals with this by empowering the peasants, while the neoliberal option proposes a shift to agribusiness.

This neoliberal option is now being vigorously implemented. Laws preventing the sale of this land have been rescinded. Meanwhile governmental aid to ejidal production has been reduced, and products of U.S. agribusiness are now imported without tariffs. This has made the situation of the peasants still more difficult and encourages them to sell their land at low prices. This, in turn, is designed to attract agribusiness from the United States to invest in this land.

There is little doubt that these policies will result in increased production and export of Mexican agricultural products to the United States. The land in question has not been abused as has most of the agribusiness land in the United States; and Mexican labor is much cheaper. Hence, moving operations to Mexico will be highly profitable for U.S. companies.

Some of the peasant proprietors whose land is bought for this purpose will be employed on the new estates, but most will not. Probably more will be displaced than can be employed in the new maquiladoras. Pressure to migrate to the United States is likely to increase. In any case, exports will increase, thus enabling Mexico to make payments on its debts.

Meanwhile, U.S. capital is able to buy Mexican businesses or to compete with them by establishing new ones. The results, it is expected, will be greater efficiency in the way business is carried on in Mexico. Mexican business will become "leaner and meaner." This means that fewer people will be employed per unit of production, and the number of Mexican small businesses will decline. *Newsweek* reported that already in early 1992 one-third of the toy makers of Mexico had been put out of business by competition with mass-produced toys from the United States.[2] This is a minor example, but it is indicative of the kind of changes that are being sought.

The cost of goods within Mexico should decline, and the variety should increase. Standards of environmental protection will probably improve somewhat, at least for a while. These are the expected results of enlarging markets. On the other side, the ownership of land and business by individual Mexicans will decline, wages will remain very low, and governmental services for the poor will be minimal.

At present, and in the short-term future, there is little doubt that increased trade will increase the suffering of the poor. This is what restructuring is all about. Free trade advocates insist that this is a temporary situation. They believe that as production increases, all Mexicans will benefit. The hope is for trickle down on a massive scale.

But, will the increase of Mexico's GNP that these policies are already achieving reduce the suffering of the poor? If they so increase employment that labor becomes scarce relative to demand, then no doubt wages will rise significantly. But is this likely to happen? Simple projections of present tendencies show that although there may be some increase in employment, it will not be rapid. The loss of work in agriculture, handicrafts, and small enterprises with little capital, together with the constant effort of industry to increase productivity so as to reduce its employment of labor, suggest that a great increase in job opportunities even at current depressed wages cannot be expected. Meanwhile, the labor force grows rapidly. It is hard to project a time when labor will be in short supply in Mexico!

The most optimistic projections are for an improvement of 5 percent a year in wages. At that rate it would take many years for the minimum wage to return to the $1.50 level from which it was reduced in restructuring. In any case, this *is* optimistic. Should the government raise wages much, or impose other costs on manufacturing, industry will have an incentive to move to other countries that will be competing for U.S. investments. With negotiations already under way with other Latin American governments, this is hardly a hypothetical prospect.

How are Christians to appraise the two developmental options outlined by Goulet? Four principles are relevant to this appraisal. First, Christians are particularly concerned about the effects of policies on the poor. Second, Christians support the principle of subsidiarity, that decisions should be made at the lowest possible level. Third, Christians believe human beings need healthy community. Fourth, Christians are concerned about the well-being of the people as a whole over time.

By his description, what Goulet calls the nationalistic option is better for the poor and keeps decisions closer to the people affected by them. It is oriented to empowering more people to attain their basic needs with dignity and participation. Hence, Christians must inevitably look favorably on this option with respect to the first two principles.

The relevance of the third principle is almost equally obvious. The process of industrialization involved in the neoliberal option is embodied most vividly in the maquiladoras. The workers have left their homes and their extended families to live in shanty towns along the Rio Grande. The new communities formed there are initially far inferior to the ones from which they have come; and alas, they have little prospect of developing into healthy ones. The industrialization of agriculture will do to the Mexican countryside what has been done in the United States since World War II. Thousands of villages will disappear, and the surplus population will move to urban slums, to the maquiladoras, or as illegal immigrants, to the United States. The decline of community involved in these shifts is apparent.

The more difficult question is whether the neoliberal option would lead to greater well-being of the people as a whole over time. Those who favor this option argue that only their policies can lead to general prosperity in the long run. These arguments are worthy of serious consideration.

Economists have long shown that expanding the size of markets tends to increase production within them. This happens for two reasons. First, in a larger geographical area there are more choices for locating production and, therefore, greater likelihood that conditions will be favorable to efficiency. Second, the larger the market, the greater the specialization that is possible; and the greater the specialization, the greater the productivity. Although these principles need to be qualified in some respects, I will assume their general validity and agree that enlarging the market to include Canada, the United States, and Mexico in a single free-trade zone will tend to increase the overall production of goods and services.

This means that free trade tends to increase GNP. For many people, including Christians, this translates directly into the idea that it improves economic welfare in general. For them, therefore, the question we are asking here is answered. In their view, if neoliberal policies, including free trade, achieve faster economic growth than the nationalistic policies described by Goulet, then, whatever the costs in other respects, these contribute more to economic welfare. Usually economic welfare seems so important that Christians who identify it with GNP conclude that we should support these neoliberal policies in general while trying to mitigate the suffering they engender.

However, economists know that the equation of per capita GNP and economic welfare is false. GNP includes many items that do not enhance welfare. For example, threats against national security raise military expenditures and thus increase the GNP, but shifting resources from consumer goods to military armaments is unfavorable to economic welfare. As crime increases, the GNP rises because of the additional expenditures on police, the legal system, and the jails, but this does not mean that the people as a whole are better off economically.

Economists speak of defensive expenditures to refer to those that are required because of changes in society or the environment rather than directly contributing to greater consumption of desired goods. In addition to national defense and defense against crime, they include many other costs of social change. In general the shift from a subsistence agricultural economy to an urban-industrial one requires enormous expenditures to make urban life possible and to deal with the social problems it generates. All of these add to the GNP. But they are in fact costs of industrialization. Today, as pollution becomes a major problem, for example, many expenditures are required to restrict and protect against it.

Actually, economists understand most governmental expenditures to be defensive. Hence, when they are measuring welfare rather than total market activity, they leave out most governmental costs. They begin their calculations of economic welfare with personal consumption rather than total product.

Although personal consumption is much less than total product, this change does not have much effect on overall judgments about policies in developed countries. There the two tend to increase at about the same rate. In the United States since World War II, personal consumption has remained consistently about two-thirds of GNP. Hence, although this shift affects the figures used, the rate of increase remains little changed. This means that judgments made on the basis of GNP tend to hold up when measured against personal consumption instead, at least in industrialized countries.

However, there are more serious problems with using GNP to measure economic welfare. GNP measures throughput, that is, it indicates how rapidly resources are being consumed and turned into wastes. It does not take account of the reduction of resources or the creation of pollution. But true economic welfare must be sustainable economic welfare. In other words, a family cannot be considered well off economically if it is using up its savings at a rapid rate. And a nation should not be thought of as prospering if it is using up its resources rapidly and projecting on the future the cost of dealing with its wastes. A measure of sustainable economic welfare must consider this.

Thus far we have been considering what should be subtracted from GNP if we are to arrive at a welfare measure. There are also positive contributions to economic welfare that are not included in the GNP. The most important and widely recognized of these is household work. One major element in the modernization of an economy is a shift from household production to the market, in short, from what is not counted in GNP to what is. (In the United States a figure for farm products consumed on the farm *is* included.) This means that economic welfare may not be increasing as rapidly as GNP figures indicate.

In the United States, we can think of this in terms of what happens when a woman joins her husband in the work force. Her earnings are counted as pure gain in GNP calculations. However, if there is a shift from eating at home to eating in restaurants, if someone is hired to clean the house or take care of children, and if house repairs are now done by professionals, the actual gain in economic welfare of the family may be considerably less.

In some traditional societies, market transactions are still a minor part of the actual production that meets the needs of the people. When peasant self-sufficiency is replaced by agribusiness, the increase in GNP cannot all be considered as gain in economic welfare.

There are other considerations relevant to welfare that may be either positive or negative. In the case of a family, we would consider that its sustainable economic situation is improving when it saved money, even though this required some belt-tightening. The sustainable economic welfare of the family would be considered in decline even if it lived extravagantly but financed its expenditures by borrowing. However, not *all* borrowing by a family would count against its sustainable well-being. If it borrowed in order to develop a successful family business, for example, this might even enhance its sustainable economic welfare.

The same principles apply to nations. Economists have tended to think of national borrowing as being for the sake of economic development and hence have not counted it as a negative factor. However, the United States has been borrowing not for investment but for consumption. Accordingly, its growing debt, as well as its sale of assets to other nations, counts against its sustainable economic welfare. For the lending nations, on the other hand, these considerations would add to their sustainable economic welfare.

Finally, Christians, at least, will not consider that economic welfare is improving if only the rich are getting richer. An increasing gap between the rich and the poor reflects a decline in real welfare. But the GNP does not consider such matters, and, as we have seen, policies designed to increase the GNP often worsen the position of the poor, at least relatively, and sometimes absolutely.

For these reasons, among others, before we assume that policies geared to increasing per capita GNP are better for improving the overall well-being of the people over time, we should consider a better way of calculating economic welfare. A group of us have developed an Index of Sustainable Economic Welfare (ISEW) for this purpose, as already discussed in chapter 3. The ISEW takes account of all the elements mentioned above and others in the United States from 1950 through 1990.[3] Because no comparable calculations have been done for Mexico, no specific conclusions about welfare changes there can be drawn. Nevertheless, a comparison of GNP and ISEW changes in the United States can provide data to challenge the validity of the widespread tendency among Christians to support policies designed to increase the GNP on the assumption that they also improve economic welfare.

The GNP per capita doubled in the United States in the forty years from 1951 to 1990. During that period, the ISEW per capita increased only 17 percent. In the last ten years of the period covered, while the GNP per capita rose by 17 percent, the ISEW per capita actually fell by 4 percent.

These statistics establish the point that continuing to pursue policies designed simply to increase GNP is unlikely to improve sustainable economic welfare in the United States. Meanwhile, those policies appear to have other negative effects that cannot be measured in dollars. For example, numerous communities have been destroyed by the enlargement of farms and numerous others by factory closings. This record in the United States provides no warrant to suppose that the long-term welfare of the Mexican people will be best secured by similar (indeed, more extreme) policies. The chances are good that the nationalistic path would enhance welfare much more, including sustainable economic welfare.

I began by focusing on Mexico, where Christians should support the nationalistic type of development rather than the neoliberal one. This does not mean that, for Mexico's sake, there should be no trade between Mexico and the United States. That would be ridiculous. But trade policies should be geared to the realization of the goals described by Goulet. Such trade would not be free from governmental control. If we are concerned about the real interests of the people of Mexico, we will oppose free trade between the United States and Mexico. Now that NAFTA is in place, this will be very difficult. But we must still support nationalistic development in Mexico, however opposed this is to the policies of its present government.

Should Mexico ever adopt the nationalist policy outlined by Goulet, it might not be able to repay its international debts. This would require some financial sacrifice on the part of the United States. There can be little doubt that the dominant economic powers have forced restructuring on so many Third World countries mainly from a desire to collect payments from them. If they follow nationalist policies of economic development, many debts will never be paid. Although forgiving such debts would not be a major financial crisis in the United States, there would be significant costs. Does this constitute a good reason for supporting free trade despite the sacrifices this imposes on the poor of Mexico?

I do not think so. I can apply only common sense here, but I do not see that the United States really benefits by continuing and increasing its massive trade deficits. Yet the only way that debtor nations can pay their debts is by having a favorable trade balance. This requires us to have an unfavorable one, which may not prove healthy for the U.S. economy.

The most obvious effects of free trade in the United States are a reduction of well-paying industrial jobs. Factories that pay good wages to union labor are not able to compete with factories that have moved to Mexico (or to other low-wage countries). They either move or lose out in the competition or, as a third possibility, cut wages. Examples of all three eventualities abound. As a result, the average wage in this country has been declining since 1980. Even official U.S. government sources project some continuing decline as a result of continuing and intensifying free-trade policies.

How far will this decline go? Optimists believe that free trade will increase our exports to Mexico and that this will create new—and relatively well-paid—jobs in the United States. No doubt some of this will occur. But even the optimists recognize that these will be jobs in businesses in which wages are a small part of expenses, that is, businesses that do not employ many workers. It is unlikely that the newly created positions will balance the losses. Indeed, it is hard to see what in the neoliberal program will stop the free fall of wages.

If we consider not simply wages but also the role and status of labor in the United States, the results are still more negative. The freedom of capital to move across borders has already severely weakened the labor movement. A relatively immobile national labor force cannot compete on an equal basis with freely mobile international capital. The farther we go in the direction of free trade, the more unequal this contest becomes. Those who live from capital become richer. Those who live from labor become poorer.

Supporters of NAFTA have argued that because the United States has a favorable balance of trade with Mexico, it will import more from us as it becomes more prosperous. This will create new jobs in this country. Usually they fail to note that much of our recent export to Mexico has been factories! Now that NAFTA is in effect, this export of our factories will no doubt continue. But this does not carry with it the reassurance that is suggested.

One way of assessing what has happened in recent years as a result of the mobility of capital is by looking at our society's inability to meet social needs. Both the federal and state governments are finding it more difficult to meet these needs now than they did earlier. It is foolish to treat this as a temporary consequence of recession, since the difficulty increased throughout a decade in which the GNP was growing rapidly.

The reasons for this increased difficulty in meeting basic human needs go beyond the enormous waste on military expenditures and the corruption of our financial institutions. First, although restructuring has not been forced on us, the neoliberal policies we have adopted for the sake of economic growth have increased the need for social services for the poor while reducing funding for this purpose. Second, people whose real wages are declining become increasingly resentful of taxes. Third, competition for industry forces concessions that mean that, instead of communities deriving taxes from industry, tax money is often spent to attract industry. Fourth, internationally mobile capital can largely avoid local and even national taxation.

Fifth, we have compounded these problems, rooted in the increasingly global economic system, by intentionally undertaxing the rich in hopes that their investments would stimulate the economy, while doing nothing to ensure that those investments would be made productively in the national economy. Despite some improvement under the Democratic administration, these inequities continue.

Although not all of these points relate directly to free trade, several of them do. Capital mobility is a major source of the problem. As long as the goods produced abroad are restricted in their entry into the United States, there are some limits to the damage done by this mobility. But when, as with Mexico, the goods can be brought back into the United States with little or no cost, then the incentive for companies to invest in the U.S. economy is still further reduced.

Against all of these objections, it is typically asserted that our economy must become globally competitive if we are to survive. This justifies lowering wages and standards for both workers and the environment. It justifies reducing subsidies to the poor. It justifies moving capital abroad and allowing mergers that reduce competition within the United States. It has justified the industrialization of U.S. agriculture. In general, it justifies the concentration of economic power in fewer and fewer hands.

Given certain assumptions, it remains true that we must do all these things to be globally competitive. If we are committed to global free trade, then we can survive in the ensuing competition only by taking steps such as these. Indeed, we will have to go much further than we have yet considered. But this argument is almost tautologous. Because we are destined to be in a world market, we must adopt those policies that make us competitive in such a market. It does not consider the alternative that we reverse direction and adopt goals more like the nationalist ones Goulet proposed for Mexico.

Thus far I have spoken of Mexico and the United States with NAFTA in view. But this is only part of the picture. The United States has taken the lead in the Uruguay round of the General Agreement on Tariffs and Trade (GATT), which aims to move as far as possible and as rapidly as possible toward a global free market. The issue we face, therefore, is not a specific treaty proposal but the desirability of extending free trade in general.

At this point the meaning of free trade should be articulated directly. What or who is free from what? Capital is free from control by political entities. More concretely, transnational corporations are free from restriction by national governments. In short, global power passes from political to economic control.

Some people may be so cynical about political processes that they are ready for this shift of power to take place, preferring business efficiency to political waste. However, such a position is not open to Christians. We cannot favor transferring power to persons whose responsibility is to a small group of stockholders rather than to the wider public. Our task is to empower the poor. While this is difficult enough in democratic political systems, it is impossible in transnational corporations.

Free trade means that capital is invested wherever it is most efficiently, that is, most profitably, employed, regardless of political boundaries. Since political entities and the people they represent have no power to control these investments, they must instead compete for them by making themselves attractive to the investors. This requires that they compete against all other peoples within the free market. Much of the competition consists in offering low wages, docile workers, few safety standards, and low requirements for protecting the environment. The lowering of standards in all these respects is not an accidental accompaniment of free trade. It is built into the concept.

To avoid extreme excesses, governments favoring free

trade in general may still seek some restrictions. The new GATT proposes that an existing organization in Rome, called Codex Alimentarius, should harmonize food safety standards globally. This group represents primarily those interests that seek to restrict trade as little as possible. Accordingly, their current standards are *far* lower than those of the United States.

GATT is being transformed into the World Trade Organization (WTO) and will have overall responsibility for settling trade disputes, such as Mexico's objection to the U.S. restrictions on importing tuna caught in ways that slaughter dolphins. The existing GATT decided in Mexico's favor in this instance, although Mexico withdrew its complaint to avoid derailing NAFTA. The WTO will have the authority on issues of this sort to overturn local, state, and national laws throughout the world. We can be sure that global standardization of environmental legislation will be at a low level.

Given the commitment to a global economy, the only alternative to turning over power to specialized economic institutions would be a real world government through which the will of the majority could come to expression. In theory such a government could establish worldwide standards that would regulate business activity everywhere for the good of the whole. This would be preferable to leaving the most important decisions affecting human destiny in the hands of corporations. But it is hard to be optimistic about the extent to which people would feel any genuine participation in a world government. Almost certainly such a government would be more influenced by those with the money to organize for such influence than by the masses of people. It is essential that more power be vested in world bodies, but the principle of subsidiarity calls for maintaining as much power as possible at local levels. That requires that the economy also be basically local.

The major argument in favor of a global market is that it

will increase global production. Let us assume that it does. Is this the proper goal of public policy? I have already indicated that the increase of global production is by no means guaranteed to improve economic welfare. If we are concerned to empower the poor and people in general to control many of their own affairs, and if we care about the stability and health of human communities, then the consequences of this neoliberal approach are profoundly negative.

There is a still more fundamental reason to reject the single-minded commitment to economic growth that is the major argument for supporting free trade. Christians have recently formulated this in terms of commitment to the integrity of creation. The limits of the capacity of the planet to sustain our abuse have already been exceeded. Our present economic activity is unsustainable. Policies primarily geared to increase this activity will only speed up the collapse of the life-supporting systems of the earth.

Those who recognize this danger call for "sustainable development," a goal defined in the *Brundtland Report*. This is an excellent phrase. Unfortunately, most of those who use it mean "sustainable *growth*," measured by GNP and achieved primarily by liberating transnational corporations from national policies. In this context the term *sustainable* becomes virtually meaningless. It may lead to treaties on particular matters such as depletion of the ozone layer, global warming, and forest cover, and these are to be celebrated. But unless concern for sustainability leads to reconceiving development in ways other than the increase of total production, it will only redirect the destruction of the planet.

Here, again, we can refer back to Goulet's nationalistic model of development. This would generate some increase in GNP in Mexico, an increase that is badly needed. But its primary goal is the well-being of the people, and especially of the poor. This can be improved disproportionately to the increased use of resources.

In the United States, sustainable development should aim to reduce the use of resources. We do not lack sufficient goods, but we use far too many of the resources of the planet to produce those goods, and then fail to get them to the people in need. We know that with far less energy we could generate all present end uses. We could reuse much that we now throw away. We could produce goods that would not need to be replaced so frequently. We could also produce goods nearer to the places they are consumed, reducing transportation and packaging.

The argument against placing our primary efforts here is that our salvation is to be found in growth. A rising tide, we are repeatedly told, raises all ships, and the rising of the tide is to be measured by GNP. But the truth is that despite or because of the rising tide, many ships sink, and that these policies will only hasten the destruction of the remaining ships in the inevitable storm.

Here is another argument in favor of following neoliberal policies: We have no choice. Other options exist, but they are politically impossible. We have already gone so far in empowering the rich and in persuading everyone else to accept the policies that benefit them that there is no possibility of changing direction. Our task as Christians is to moderate the suffering caused and to work for modifications that will slow down the destruction of the planet.

This is indeed what is known as political realism. Widespread adoption of the neoliberal economic view virtually guarantees that what is regarded as inevitable is in fact inevitable. There can be no shift to a different model of global economy as long as even those who recognize the dangers of the neoliberal one accept its inevitability.

Another reason to accept the movement toward free trade as inevitable is that the managers of public opinion are dedicated to this result. After virtual silence about NAFTA and the Uruguay round of GATT for years while these agreements were being hammered out, the dominant media turned to the vigorous promotion of NAFTA. *The New York Times*, for example, "planned a series of three advertorials presenting the positive economic and social benefits of NAFTA."[4] It actively solicited advertisers to sponsor these. It refused to include paid advertising that was adverse to NAFTA in these sections of the newspaper.[5] With the media so one-sidedly committed on the issue, it was hard to get an adequate debate on the real issues. We can expect that the new GATT will receive similar support.

The resultant, "realistic" policy, as supported by the Clinton administration, is to accept free trade in general and then to try to reduce the negative impact on labor and the environment. With respect to labor, this means that our government should retrain workers whose factories move to Mexico so that they can take positions in the anticipated expansion in other sectors of the economy—assuming that our national budget will allow for the increases required, or that funds will be transferred from other expenditures, or that we will further increase the national debt. It also assumes that there really will be jobs in other sectors for which the laid-off workers can train. Past experience indicates that even if there are, they will pay much less.

It will not be difficult to get political promises to the effect that workers will be retrained. But in a time when all such programs are under acute budgetary pressure, great suffering is very likely to result. The side agreement on labor puts pressure on Mexico to enforce its labor laws, but this will do little to alleviate the problem of labor in the United States.

With respect to the environment, the prospects for some gains may be a bit brighter. At least temporarily, the government of Mexico is willing to budget for the beginning of clean-up work on the Rio Grande and for more inspectors to reduce future pollution by U.S. companies. Much, much more is required, and now that NAFTA is in place, the incentive for strict regulations and massive expenditures will decline. Nevertheless, one can hope. Even the rich do not enjoy environmental decay.

It is also possible, although highly unlikely, that there can be rules governing trade that will enable the United States to refuse to import products that do not meet its own standards in terms of food safety. And it is possible that pressure by environmentalists can raise the environmental standards set by Codex Alimentarius and the new WTO. In short, continuing strenuous efforts may counteract some of the environmental losses inherent in free trade.

If our only choices are free trade with some mitigation of its destructive effects and free trade with no such mitigation, then Christians should certainly support the former, modest though the gains are likely to be. Perhaps we can salve our consciences even if we make little difference with respect to the suffering of the world's poor and have little effect on the rate of global self-destruction. But we should know that we are then not even protesting the calamitous policies that shape our destiny.

If one finds oneself on a train speeding down a hill toward a bridge that has been destroyed, what is the realistic thing to do? Let us suppose that most of the people on the train do not know that the bridge is out and that there are powerful interests committed to maintaining their ignorance. The passengers are eager to reach their destinations on the other side of the gorge that the bridge crosses. They favor moving on as rapidly as possible and resent any suggestion that the train should be slowed, much less stopped. Many of those who have reason to suspect that the bridge is out prefer not to think about it. To stop the train and take the long detour to the destination would require actions that would jolt the passengers and be quite disruptive of their plans.

Perhaps realism dictates that one should be silent and do what one can to make the remainder of the time pass pleasantly. After all, the chances of stopping the train in time are quite small given the lack of interest of those on board. But realism may not make a lot of sense in this context. It may be better to try to stop the train before it reaches the gorge, however unlikely one is to succeed. If so, the first step will be to persuade the realists on board to share in the effort.

My analogy is, of course, an alarmist one, and it is not fashionable to be an alarmist. Even those who see that our movement toward a global economy causes some problems are likely to find my cataclysmic analogy misleading. And, indeed, it is. In the analogy there is a single catastrophe awaiting the train. In the real world a continuing single-minded emphasis on increasing production will lead to many smaller catastrophes, most of which will be explained in terms of particular local circumstances rather than attributed to global policies. Most of the suffering will be borne by the invisible poor, whereas we who make public opinion and shape policy will be largely unscathed for some time to come. Where we, the rich, will obviously share in the suffering, as with the destruction of the ozone layer, actions will be taken to contain the damage.

Step by step, we will get accustomed to decaying societies in an increasingly degraded environment, and we will accept the argument that bad as the situation is, any alternative course of action would make it worse. In my perception, this ongoing deterioration is analogous to the destroyed bridge over the chasm. NAFTA and the Uruguay round of GATT are not themselves the cause of this deterioration. They are logical steps in that set of neoliberal policies that is undermining the traditional social fabric around the world, the possibility of empowering the poor, and the hope for an attractive world for our descendants.

Whereas it is difficult for us as citizens of the United States to do much directly in opposition to the restructuring programs imposed on weak debtor countries by the International Monetary Fund, we *can* work against the whole pattern by opposing U.S. leadership in promoting free trade. It is not entirely unrealistic to believe that such efforts will eventually lead to change.

It is possible, indeed, that the discussion generated around NAFTA and GATT can be expanded, despite powerful opposition, to raise more basic issues about the nature of the world economy. If people around the world understood that they now need to choose between the two models outlined by Goulet, a constituency for the nationalist choice would arise. Furthermore, if significant segments of the intelligentsia would devote their attention to examining the policies needed in each country to empower the poor, implement the principle of subsidiarity, stabilize and strengthen human community, and develop a sustainable relation to the rest of the planet, progress toward those goals could be made rapidly.

Obviously the entrenched powers that support current neoliberal policies would not yield easily. Thus far they have been able to squelch all opposition. Perhaps the realist is correct that their power is too great to challenge. But it is hard to think of that kind of realism as a Christian option.

6

The New
World Order

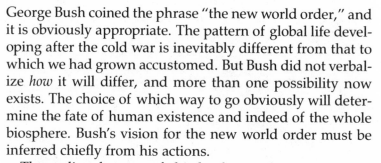

George Bush coined the phrase "the new world order," and it is obviously appropriate. The pattern of global life developing after the cold war is inevitably different from that to which we had grown accustomed. But Bush did not verbalize *how* it will differ, and more than one possibility now exists. The choice of which way to go obviously will determine the fate of human existence and indeed of the whole biosphere. Bush's vision for the new world order must be inferred chiefly from his actions.

The earlier chapters of this book articulate suggestions for a new world order based on relatively self-sufficient local economies, but this proposal is not now being discussed by those who are making basic political decisions. The Democrats seem to be following in the direction laid down by former presidents Reagan and Bush, with valuable, but minor, modifications. It is important that we be quite clear what this direction is. It has two main elements: the enlargement of markets moving toward a fully integrated global economy, and the role of the United States as global police officer to establish Pax Americana.

The primary expressions of the first of these elements are the North American Free Trade Agreement (NAFTA) and the Uruguay round of the General Agreement on Tariffs and Trade (GATT). Negotiating these and getting them approved was the heart of the Republican economic policy during the past two administrations, and President Clinton is committed to completing the job. The most obvious negative result of reducing barriers to trade is that U.S. capital invests in places where labor costs are much lower and then ships the goods back to U.S. consumers. Half a million jobs have already gone to Mexico, and perhaps another million to other low-wage areas, such as Southeast Asia. Agreements with the kind of impact possessed by NAFTA and GATT accelerate this process.

Supporters of these agreements assure us that new jobs will be created in the United States, even that more jobs will be created than will be lost. These assurances are based on faith in certain economic theories rather than on the evidence of the past decade. There is a minor difference here between most Republicans and most Democrats. The former believe that the free market will miraculously create high-paying jobs, make U.S. industry competitive, and correct our huge trade imbalance. The Democrats believe that government needs to work with industry to help it become competitive and provide the needed jobs. Neither party acknowledges that there is an inherent tendency within any market to equalize wages, so that including Mexico in the same market will continue the tendency for U.S. wages to fall toward Mexico's levels, a process that already has started to happen as capital has become globally mobile.

Proponents of these policies also argue that although some further sacrifice may be required of U.S. labor, less-developed countries, whose needs are greater, will benefit. Here, too, we are dealing more with faith in theories than with historical evidence. Factually, in order to attract export-oriented investment, the Mexican government has participated in the restructuring that is pushed on debtor countries, other than the United States, by the International Monetary Fund and the World Bank. Restructuring means lowering wages and reducing social services. Mexican wages, like those in the United States, are lower now than fifteen years ago, and, on the whole, working conditions are worse.

The beneficiaries of this aspect of the new world order are those who live on the investments. Capital is more profitable when it can move freely around the world. This freedom of capital reduces job security everywhere and forces workers to compete with other workers in other parts of the world where the cost of subsistence is less. In general, wages can be expected to rise only when labor becomes globally scarce—not a very likely outcome given present trends in population growth and the automation of industry.

Laborers are not the only casualty here; the environment also suffers. This loss takes two forms. First, integration of the global economy will, to some extent, increase overall production. This, in turn, will increase the use of natural resources and the pollution of the environment.

In response, defenders of the new world order argue that production can be increased in a sustainable way, and certainly many improvements in energy efficiency and pollution reduction are possible. Some of these improvements are also profitable and thus encouraged by market forces. But others will not be made without governmental regulation and tax policies, which the global market enables industry to escape by moving to countries that are more interested in growth than in a clean environment. For example, the U.S. factories built along the Mexican side of the Rio Grande have escaped regulations in the United States. As a result, they have turned that river into a chemical sewer. There is little reason to expect the growth associated with a globally integrated economy to be benign.

In any case, the world can endure very little additional growth, even of a benign sort. The question of when we will encounter limits is wrongly formulated. We have already gone beyond the limits of sustainable life on this planet in many identifiable ways. The need now is to reduce the impact of the economy on the environment. This can be accompanied by improvements in agriculture, some increase in certain types of industrial production, and a great deal of growth in services. But channeling growth in such ways is incompatible with the globally integrated economy toward which present policies are moving us.

The focus of policymakers should be on how to meet the basic human needs of all with minimum damage to the environment. Present policies call for improving the condition of the poor by vastly increasing the wealth of the rich. Long before even the most basic human needs are met in this way, the biosphere will collapse. Or, more realistically, the costs of responding to environmental damage will exceed the increased income made available by a growing economy, so that even the rich will be impoverished by the policies designed to make them richer.

The second way in which the new world order as now envisioned threatens the environment is that it creates organs with the power to override environmental legislation believed to restrain trade. The new World Trade Organization (WTO) that is to supersede GATT will adjudicate international disputes for the sake of facilitating the free flow of goods and services across national boundaries. All member nations must set aside any laws found discriminatory by WTO. The willingness of national governments, including our own, to give such a group, not accountable to the world's people, the power to veto both the laws of the nation and those of individual states is astonishing. It shows how far we have gone from nationalism to what I call economism, that is, subordinating all other interests to the goal of economic growth.

The military is the second major area shaping the new world order. With the end of the cold war, the reason for developing a huge defense establishment has disappeared. Given its possession of such an establishment and the changed global situation, what should the United States do?

This issue plunges us into the heart of the current American debate. The United States has built up an enormous defense establishment, including an industry that supports our military, ostensibly because of real threats from the Soviet Union. Careful studies have shown again and again that much of this expenditure was not in fact required in order to defend ourselves and allies from any such threat. But the American public was willing to sacrifice much because of its perception of real danger.

Now that it is clear to all that no such threat exists, the apparent logic would be to cut our defense expenditures drastically. The Center for Defense Information estimates that about one-third of present expenditures would suffice for defense. But it turns out that our present military budget is so central to our economy that we cannot reduce it rapidly without severe economic and social disruptions. We are forced to recognize that past decisions narrowly circumscribe our present choices.

The fundamental choice was the decision, for the first time in the history of this country, to remain prepared for war in peacetime. This choice was made in the aftermath of World War II in recognition of the power and expansionist threat of the Soviet Union. As a result, one part of our industry, instead of reverting to peacetime production, was placed on a permanent military footing. A second choice, made by Robert McNamara, secretary of defense during the Kennedy administration, was to install "an industrial management... to control the nation's largest network of industrial enterprises."[1]

Thus the United States developed, alongside its market

economy, a large command economy geared to military production. This means that much of American industry is just as unaccustomed to market competition as is that of the former Soviet Union. Furthermore, as our defense establishment is downsized, we face many of the same problems experienced by Eastern Europe in shifting from a bureaucratically managed economy to a competitive one. An eminently sensible solution would be to allow American industry to serve the civilian needs of Americans by converting this industry to civilian production. Unfortunately, for the most part, it cannot be readily done in the present context, as the following example will illustrate.

The United States now imports half of its machine tools. Seymour Melman and Lloyd J. Dumas propose that plants now producing unneeded armaments be converted to producing machine tools.[2] While this is technically feasible, these machine tools presumably would have to be sold in competition with those offered on the international market. If experienced American machine-tool manufacturers, accustomed to the competitive market, have been unable to hold their own against international competitors, how could newcomers to the field, who have never had to deal with this kind of competition, be expected to succeed? The management of most defense industries knows that this kind of conversion is hopeless and resists discussing how it can be done.

Given the context of global free trade, conversion is not a realistic option for most defense contractors. These factories must either close or be kept busy in the protected context of military production. Present policies envision a slow reduction in defense spending, with Democrats proposing that this be slightly faster than envisioned by the Republicans.

These modest reductions leave us spending money on armaments for which there is no need. But even so they are painfully disruptive. In an economy in which unemployment is a serious problem, the result will be further layoffs. Betty G. Lall and Joan Tepper Marlin calculate the probable effects on unemployment of reduced military spending.

> If defense spending (in FY 1990 dollars) were to be cut from $300 billion to $175 billion within ten years, a $12.5-billion-a-year reduction, it would mean an average decline of about 6 percent a year and *an average reduction of 362,000 defense jobs per year.* Of the layoffs, typically 14 percent, or approximately 51,000 workers, would be taken care of by attrition . . . , two-thirds of the remaining 312,000 . . . would be re-employed by the end of the fourth month. The net increase in unemployment after four months would be 104,000 workers.[3]

Adding a hundred thousand workers a year to our unemployment roles for ten years is not a happy prospect. However, my own judgment is that this understates the problem. For example, consider "attrition." In academia during recent years much of the reduction of faculty in my field is by attrition. That is, professors retire and are not replaced, or at least not replaced by full-time teachers. We may say that this does not add to unemployment, since the senior professors are retired rather than unemployed. But failure to replace adds greatly to the lack of satisfactory jobs for junior scholars. Many are forced to compete for work in the general labor market. Somewhere along the line this *does* add to unemployment.

Also, the assumption that two-thirds would find employment within four months comes from experience in contexts in which there is not a steady erosion of industry caused both by the decline of defense production and the movement of production overseas. It impresses me as optimistic. In any case, the new jobs in most instances will pay less than the old ones.

I am describing the very serious bind in which this country finds itself. It cannot afford to continue the huge military expenditures that have caused the accumulation of enormous debt and keep cutting back on important human services and infrastructure expenditures. Since the people have no need for most of this production, it seems sensible to shift expenditures elsewhere and reduce the debt. But in the process of doing this in a globally integrated economy, the already acute problem of unemployment will grow worse. The reduced revenues from taxes and increased costs of unemployment compensation will make more difficult the response to other needs.

In view of the negative effects of reducing military expenditures, seeking justification for maintaining a large military budget is understandable. According to the Center for Defense Information, "most of the Pentagon's request for almost $300 billion in 1993 military spending is to prepare for military action in regional struggles far from U.S. shores."[4] The proposal is that we spend nearly as much money in our new role as global police officer as we formerly did to protect the First World from the threat of the Second. Of course, this is far more than would really be needed for the new role, just as in the past we spent far more than was really needed to contain any expansionist goals of the Soviet Union. But since the primary consideration is the maintenance of a complex military-industrial establishment rather than realistic missions, this expense is understandable. And if the choice is between destroying much of our remaining industrial base or deceiving ourselves in this way, perhaps the deception is warranted.

The second major element in the new world order into which we are moving, therefore, is a Pax Americana. The United States will be responsible for maintaining peace and order throughout the world wherever its own interests and those of its allies require this. Bush gave us in the Persian Gulf War an indication of how this works, and he left us a better example in Somalia. Whether our intervention there will prove to have done more good than harm remains to be seen.

The logic of the Pax Americana is closely connected with the first element of Bush's new world order. In a globally integrated economy, there must be provisions for dealing with actions of nations or within nations that threaten the smooth functioning of business and trade. Since no world government is envisioned, military power remains in the hands of the nation-states. Because the United States is now the unchallenged military superpower, the task of maintaining world order falls to us.

One could also argue against our assuming this role. First, there is the question of whether the United States (or any other nation) can be trusted with a near monopoly of power. Can we be expected to employ this for the general good? Or will national interests distort our role? As the United States has long policed the Western Hemisphere, a study of the nature of U.S. military interventions in Latin America during the past century is not reassuring.

Second, the United States cannot afford this role. Building and maintaining its military establishment has caused this nation to run up an enormous debt both internally and to other countries. Whereas it once had the highest standard of living in the world, this is no longer true. The standard still maintained requires heavy borrowing from the future. The country seems no longer able to afford quality education or services to meet the basic needs of the poor. Those nations that have devoted their resources to civilian research and production now surpass the United States in these crucial areas. In the long run, we will not be able to finance the military power that enables us to police the world. Indeed, that long run may not be so long.

The nation is caught, then, in an acute bind. Given the commitment to integration of the global economy, it cannot convert the defense industry to civilian production. Adopting the permanent role of global police officer would provide public justification for maintaining a large military establishment, which could, in fact, service the globally integrated market. But even if we set aside scruples about having controlling military power in the hands of a single nation, the United States cannot afford to maintain a huge military establishment. To try to do so will lead to continuing economic decline.

The extreme difficulty of demilitarizing the economy is closely tied to the other main feature of the emerging new world order—a globally integrated economy. The military industry has survived because it has been protected from global competition. Civilian industry within the United States is losing out in this competition, with industrial managers hoping to recoup their place in global competition by using cheap labor in other countries, especially Mexico. Massive conversion of military industry to civilian production is impossible in this context. It cannot be accomplished without the governmental protection that is incompatible with a globally integrated economy.

There is a solution, but it would require moving toward a different world order. If the United States made a healthy national economy its priority, instead of subordinating this to an integrated global economy, then much military industry could be converted into producing goods now imported from other parts of the world. This nation could become, once again, industrially self-sufficient. Much of the research now directed to weapons of mass destruction could be redirected to improving efficiency in the use of energy, in recycling, and in small-scale local production, and replacing decaying infrastructure with new environmentally benign alternatives. Long-term research can continue to be governmentally supported during a gradual transition to entry into the competitive national market. There would be no need to invent new missions to justify the maintenance of an industry that produces nothing of human value. Overall production might decline, but production for human use would rise.

Calculating on contemporary assumptions, the proposal that overall production in this country would decline implies that there would be an increase of unemployment. Indeed, it is generally supposed that unemployment can only be kept low by rapid growth in production. Since that growth requires that each business become "leaner and meaner," that is, employ fewer people and at lower wages, the goal of full employment remains elusive.

In a national economy in which companies must compete only with other companies operating with the same rules and requirements, there are other possibilities. For example, whereas the focus in the past has been on substituting fossil fuels for labor, thereby making labor more productive, a national economy could focus on economizing fossil fuels even when this made some forms of production more labor intensive. A shift of direction is particularly important in the agricultural sector, where soil should also be economized, even if more labor would be required to produce an equal amount of food.

I am making the case for national economies over a globally integrated one in terms of the issues we are facing in the aftermath of the cold war—the shaping of a new world order. I believe strongly that both of the elements in that new world order to which this nation seems to be committed are pernicious. But one could well argue that a return to nationalism is also pernicious. This is true. And it is the ugly history of nationalism that makes a third option attractive to many.

A third possible new world order differs both from the one I am proposing and from the one that is actually coming into being. My proposal is for decentralizing both political and economic power, always keeping the political power dominant. The policy to which our government is committed frees economic power from political power, turning over controlling power in the world to those who own capital. The third possibility is to centralize both economic and political power. This requires the development of a world government with sufficient power to control an integrated global economy so that it will serve the interests of the human community.

My own judgment is that this is not a desirable direction. I believe that some of our global problems must be dealt with globally, and for this reason I favor much more concentration of power at the global level than we now have. But I believe that whatever decisions can be made locally should be made there. I do not trust a centralized global government to be sensitive to the highly diverse human and ecological needs all around the planet. And I believe that removing still further from ordinary human beings and their communities the power to order their own lives can lead only to an intensification of alienation and dehumanization.

Furthermore, all actual historical experience indicates that those with sufficient resources will be able to have a very disproportionate influence on the way a centralized government makes its decisions. Although constitutionally such a government might have the power to regulate economic interests to political ends, in fact it would almost certainly be influenced primarily by those economic interests. We know how far this has gone in the United States. In all probability it would be even more true of a global government. Citizen efforts to correct this distortion would have little chance of success.

Of the three options I have outlined, I believe that the worst is the one the United States is now pursuing. I see no justification for turning over decision-making power to those who are accountable only to the very rich. The people who make these decisions in transnational corporations are no worse and no better than the rest of us. I am not attacking them. I would not want any small group of us to be entrusted with such power even if we were accountable to the public. Even more certainly I do not want such power turned over to people who are *not* accountable to those who are radically affected by its use.

World government is preferable to this. It would at least have the formal structures that would enable those affected by its decisions to exert some influence upon it. If we must have a global economy, then we must have a world government to set its parameters. But I fear this kind of global centralization of both economic and political power.

The argument for nationalism opposes both a globally integrated economy and a world government. At present the nation-states are the only possible sources of resistance to this centralization of power in the hands of transnational corporations. My real goal, however, is not nationalism but decentralization. The principle advocated is one that has been articulated many times in the history of Christian political ethics, especially by Catholics. It is called "subsidiarity."

The principle of subsidiarity means that governments at higher levels are subsidiary to those at lower levels. In other words, decisions should be made at the smallest or most local level possible. Families should have the freedom to make many decisions about their life together and their place in the world. Of course, families must work with other families in villages, towns, or neighborhoods to create institutions that meet their shared needs, and much governance should be located there. But again, at least in industrialized societies, small communities of this sort cannot meet all their own needs. They must group together in counties or cities, and these in states or provinces, and these in nations, and these in regions. Finally, there are many decisions that can only be made at the global level. The global level of political organization exists to serve the regions of which it is composed; the regions, the nations; the nations, the states or provinces; and so forth down to the most local level.

The point is that power should be conceived as belonging to the people organized in families and that the communities in which they group themselves derive their power, as stated in the Declaration of Independence, "from the consent of the governed." Power should be transferred to larger communities of communities only as this is needed for the common good. What can be decided and done locally should be decided and done there, except when this makes it more difficult for other localities. When actions in one locale adversely affect others, or when what is needed requires a larger base to occur, communities of communities should be the locale of power and action—and then communities of communities of communities.

In this picture, nations retain importance, but not absolute sovereignty. Some of their power devolves on smaller regions within the nation; some is transferred to communities of nations. On this latter point, the European Economic Community provides a remarkable model. The current danger is that for purposes of competition in a globally integrated market, the transfer of power to the larger community may go too far. For example, a single currency will lead to concentration of power in fewer hands. It would be better, instead, to maintain the past balance between individual nations and the European Community and transfer more power to smaller units within the European nations.

Since the economy is of decisive importance for human survival, its decentralization is our first concern. A town meeting is a beautiful form of participatory governance in a local community. But if that community's economy is based on companies over whose continuance or removal the community exercises no control, then the range of decisions that the town meeting can make is very limited. The removal of its economic base is likely to destroy the town regardless of the excellence of its governance. A threat to remove such companies will force the town to set aside many of its values in order to persuade the company to stay, and even this may not suffice.

Alongside the principle of subsidiarity, therefore, is a corollary. Political power responsible to the people as a whole must be able to establish the parameters within which economic power (responsible to those who profit from it) functions. Otherwise, there is no protection for the poor, or indeed for workers at any level. Also, there is no protection for the community and its environment. Thus, the application of the principle of subsidiarity depends drastically on the organization of the economy. A nationally organized economy requires the concentration of political power at the national level. A globally organized economy requires the concentration of political power at the global level. The village economies still operative in many traditional societies allow for village governance of village affairs.

I envision a decentralized economy in which even small localities would have more control of their economic life than is now possible, but in which relative self-sufficiency would be possible only in considerably larger areas. Nevertheless, in the United States, the areas that could approximate self-sufficiency would be much smaller than the nation as a whole. Hence considerable power could be moved downward to these regions.

The ideal of relative self-sufficiency does not preclude trade. It does, however, preclude what is now called "free trade." It is important to understand both how free trade was originally understood and what the term has now come to mean.

In Great Britain when the classical economists began to write, there was some truth in the idea that all participation in the market was voluntary. Often the image of Robinson

Crusoe has been used to depict the marvels of free trade. Crusoe is self-sufficient. He does not *have* to trade. But if he discovers that there is a nearby island whose inhabitants have goods he would like, and if he has some they would like, both benefit from the exchange. This is free trade in the full, original meaning of the term, which I affirm wholeheartedly. Furthermore, as long as the poor in eighteenth-century England could subsist from the commons, there was some truth in the myth that their choice to work in factories was, like Robinson's decision, a free exchange of labor for payment, which enabled them to purchase more than they could derive from the commons.

However, this myth even then distorted the historical reality. The nobility were rapidly enclosing the commons and making it impossible for the poor to subsist on the land. The choice to work in factories was still free in one sense, but the alternative was to die. An economic system that makes work on terms established by others the only alternative to death is not a truly free market.

Trade between nations is free in the ideal sense when the nations do not have to trade in order to meet their basic needs. In short, it presupposes relative self-sufficiency, which is the kind of trade I strongly favor. But in the real world, such trade has become rare.

Consider how this change occurs with the artificial example of Robinson Crusoe and his neighbors on another island. Initially, the trade is ideally free. But suppose Crusoe finds that by producing more of fewer items, he can exchange his surplus of these for more of the goods he has ceased to produce. He thereby gives up self-sufficiency for greater total consumption. This is rational activity as understood by economists.

But notice what has happened when he is no longer self-sufficient. At first, if his trading partner refuses to sell him what he needs or sets the terms of trade unfairly, he probably can return to producing all his necessities. But after a while that becomes impossible. Now his very survival depends on meeting his needs by trade. If this is not true for his trading partner, then this partner now has a great advantage. He can set the terms of trade as he pleases. Crusoe is completely at his mercy. The trade is still free in the contemporary understanding of the term, and the managers of the global economy celebrate this so-called interdependence. Crusoe can choose to starve rather than accept the terms offered him. But this is not the sort of free trade I regard as desirable.

In short, although in the current debate I oppose what is called "free trade," my concern is to restore the conditions within which trade could be truly free. When people or nations are free not to trade, then they are also in position to engage in trade freely. When they do so, it will be because it is truly to their advantage to trade. A globally integrated economy puts an end to the possibility of this authentically free trade, but a community of relatively self-sufficient communities makes such trade possible.

I am also committed to market economies. I am not proposing bureaucratic management of the economy by insisting that political governance responsible to the whole people have power over economic activities. In *For the Common Good*, Daly and I have argued at length that markets can harness the knowledge of many and work far better in the allocation of resources than can centralized control of any sort.[5] The collapse of the Communist governments of Eastern Europe only confirms what has long been apparent. Markets should be freed to do what they do well.

Nevertheless, markets should serve communities, not destroy them. Communities have not only the right but the duty to establish policies that implement their values. If they prefer good working conditions, healthy people, and a healthy environment with fewer goods, to the alternative of poor working conditions, sickly people, and a deteriorating environment with more goods, then rules restricting business in certain ways are entirely just and right.

It would be unjust and self-destructive to force producers within the jurisdiction of these rules to compete with others not bound by them. If protecting local business from such unfair competition is to be called "protectionism," then protectionism should be strongly affirmed. On the other hand, if protectionism means giving unfair advantages to some businesses over others, then it should be opposed. Unfair advantage in fact occurs when goods produced in places that do not protect their workers or their environment are allowed to compete without tariffs with goods produced under regulations established by a concerned and responsible community.

We are now moving into a world in which the United States takes on the role of global police officer. I have indicated objections to that policy and also how changing from a globally integrated to a national economy would make the rapid reduction of military spending possible. Also, a decentralized economy is not as dependent as a globally integrated one on controlling what happens all around the world. Still, problems arise in various parts of the world, such as now in Somalia and Bosnia, which call for concern and involvement from outside. If the United States does not take on the role of global police officer, how should these problems be treated?

I approach this question with the model in mind that I presented earlier, the model of communities of communities. Let us begin by considering unacceptable situations that might arise in the United States if it became a community of states or bioregions rather than a highly centralized nation. In terms of our national history, the problem to which we should be most sensitive is that in some states or regions the majority might run roughshod over minorities, denying their civil and human rights. The way I have described the model thus far offers little protection against this abuse.

Sufficient national and worldwide consensus about the importance of human rights now exists that each community of communities should be able to make the commitment to observe these rights a condition of participation. Gross violations should be punished by removal of the rights and privileges of participation in this inclusive community. In extreme cases, the larger community together with its other members might intervene militarily in the internal affairs of one of its members.

Consider a different possibility. Presumably one condition of membership in the larger community would be that the smaller community would not violate the boundaries of other members or of outside communities. Suppose that, nevertheless, war breaks out between two subcommunities. It would be appropriate for the inclusive community, together with the other subcommunities, to intervene to stop the violence and compel the parties involved to submit their disagreement to adjudication.

With a little imagination one can extend this model to larger communities of communities up to the global one. There should be sufficient power at each level, in alliance with the communities not directly involved in the conflict, to impose a solution when that seems to be the only way to ensure a modicum of justice and order. However, this, too, should be done as far as possible in the region that is most immediately affected. For example, the countries of Africa should develop sufficient strength and organization to intervene in Liberia, the Sudan, or Somalia if and when they collectively decide that this is needed. In the long run, it will be far better for interventions in African nations to be carried out by other Africans than by Americans or Europeans. If problems in Africa cannot be handled by Africans, then an appeal for help should be made to the United Nations.

These proposals are not intended to be utopian. Regional control of regional affairs will often be inept and unfair, and it will sometimes exacerbate problems rather than solve them. Regions will intervene when they should not and fail to intervene when they should. Nevertheless, if the history of intervention by the United States in Latin American countries is any indication, these distortions will not be reduced if we play the role of global police officer. Our goal is not to discover a system that will put an end to human stupidity and arrogance. It is only to develop a world order that will introduce checks on the excesses to which these lead and encourage all people to play a more responsible role in managing their own affairs, while reducing the likelihood of global disaster.

We live in a time of true opportunity and vast danger, as we move rapidly toward organizing the world in a way that will increase the danger and reduce the freedom to respond to it. If we continue in this direction, it is hard to see how humanity can avoid catastrophe. In short, the new world order heralded by Bush and thus far seconded by Clinton is an unmitigated disaster.

Before we lock ourselves into this now-emerging new world order, we have the opportunity to consider other options. I have noted two. One is the subordination of an integrated global economy to a world government. That would keep open some options for human beings to shape their destiny. But it inspires little hope in me.

The other is the one that has captured my imagination. I believe it is a truly hopeful one. Its adoption would not end the environmental crisis or the human one, but it would position humanity in such a way that intelligent responses would be possible. It is a mistake today to look for ideal solutions. There are none. But it is not a mistake to look for ways to avoid catastrophes or at least to minimize those that may now already be inevitable and to prepare to rebuild in a sustainable way. My conviction is that the decentralization of the economy and the organization of the political world in terms of communities of communities offers these possibilities.

Notes

PREFACE

1. Herman Daly and John B. Cobb, Jr., *For the Common Good: Redirecting the Economy Toward Community, the Environment, and a Sustainable Future* (Boston: Beacon Press, 1989; updated and expanded edition, 1994).

2. John B. Cobb, Jr., "Against Free Trade," *Theology and Public Policy* 4, no. 2 (fall 1992): 4–16.

3. See chapter 4, note 3.

4. James P. Grant, "A Decade of Achievement Threatened," *The State of the World's Children, 1989* (New York: Oxford University Press for UNICEF, 1989).

5. Robert D. Kaplan, "The Coming Anarchy," *Atlantic Monthly*, February 1994, 44–76.

1. CHRISTIAN FAITH AND THE DEGRADATION OF CREATION

1. Adam Smith, *An Inquiry into the Nature and Causes of the Wealth of Nations* (1776; reprinted as *The Wealth of Nations* [New York: Knopf, 1991]). For a very popular history of economics featuring Adam Smith as the key initiator of the academic disci-

pline, see Robert Heilbroner, *The Worldly Philosophers: The Lives and Times and Ideas of the Great Economic Thinkers*, 6th ed. (New York: Simon and Schuster, 1986).

2. The work of Hunter and Amory Lovins in the Rocky Mountain Institute is an especially important example. The ideas were first effectively articulated by Amory B. Lovins in *Soft Energy Paths: Toward a Durable Peace* (San Francisco: Friends of the Earth, 1977).

3. Sallie McFague has shown how this works out in *The Body of God: An Ecological Theology* (Minneapolis: Fortress, 1993).

2. ECONOMICS AND THE HUMANITIES

1. Alfred North Whitehead, *Process and Reality*, corrected edition, edited by David Ray Griffin and Donald W. Sherburne (New York: Free Press, 1978), 259.

2. Alfred North Whitehead, *Science and the Modern World* (New York: New American Library, 1925), chap. 3. In *For the Common Good*, Herman Daly and I discuss in some detail the fallacy of misplaced concreteness in economics (see especially pp. 35–43).

3. Steven E. Rhoads, *The Economist's View of the World* (New York: Cambridge University Press, 1985), 161–62. Rhoads's source is Gerald Maxwell and Ruth Ames, "Economists Free Ride, Does Anyone Else?" *Journal of Public Economics* 15 (1981): 295–310. Rhoads's is the best book I know by a noneconomist about economics.

4. Stephen E. G. Lea, Roger M. Tarpy, and Paul Webley, *The Individual in the Economy: A Survey of Economic Psychology* (New York: Cambridge University Press, 1987).

5. Lovins, *Soft Energy Paths*.

6. *Denver Post*, 7 April 1991, pp. 17A-18A.

7. Ibid., 18A.

8. Rhoads, *The Economist's View of the World*, chap. 9.

9. World Commission on Environment and Development Staff, *Our Common Future* (New York: Oxford University Press, 1987).

10. Daly and Cobb, *For the Common Good*, undertakes to advance this discussion.

3. SUSTAINABILITY AND COMMUNITY

1. Most of the work on this index has been done by Clifford Cobb. The latest version is published as an appendix in the 1994 edition of Daly and Cobb, *For the Common Good,* and in Clifford W. Cobb and John B. Cobb, Jr., *The Green National Product: A Proposed Index of Sustainable Economic Welfare* (Lanham, Md.: University Press of America, 1994).

2. Karl Polanyi, *The Great Transformation* (New York: Octagon Books, 1975).

3. Daly and Cobb, *For the Common Good,* chaps. 8, 9.

4. E. F. Schumacher, *Small Is Beautiful: Economics As If People Mattered* (New York: Harper and Row, 1973), 167. Schumacher more often used the term "intermediate technology."

5. Julie Fisher provides an overall view of these movements in *The Road from Rio: Sustainable Development and the Nongovernmental Movement in the Third World* (Westport, Conn.: Praeger Publishers, 1993).

6. This is the title of a frequently reprinted essay by Garrett Hardin. See Garrett Hardin and John Baden, eds., *Managing the Commons* (San Francisco: W. H. Freeman, 1977).

7. See, e.g., *How Big Is Our Ecological Footprint? A Handbook for Estimating a Community's Appropriated Carrying Capacity* (The Task Force on Planning Healthy and Sustainable Communities, 1993). Copies can be obtained from Janette McIntosh, Department of Family Practice, University of British Columbia, 5804 Fairview Ave., Vancouver, B.C., Canada V6T 1Z3.

8. Paolo Soleri, *Arcology: The City in the Image of Man* (Cambridge, Mass.: MIT Press, 1969).

9. At its 1982 assembly at Vancouver, the stated goal of the World Council of Churches was changed from "a just, participatory, and sustainable society" to "peace, justice, and the integrity of creation."

4. TO PAY OR NOT TO PAY?

1. Susan George, *The Debt Boomerang: How Third World Debt Harms Us All* (Boulder, Col.: Westview Press, 1992), xiv.

2. The Dag Hammarskjöld Foundation, *Another Development: Approaches and Strategies* (Uppsala, Sweden: DHF, 1977), 10.

3. Paul Ekins, *A New World Order: Grassroots Movements for Social Change* (London: Routledge, 1992), 88–99. Other examples of World Bank projects that have been humanly and environmentally destructive can be found in Bruce Rich, *Mortgaging the Earth: The World Bank, Environmental Impoverishment, and the Crisis of Development* (Boston: Beacon Press, 1993). There has been some improvement in World Bank policies. For example, in the summer of 1991 in its Forest Policy Paper, it pledged it "will not under any circumstances" finance commercial logging in primary tropical moist forests ("World Bank Adopts New Forest Policy," *World Bank News,* May 1992, 34). This new responsiveness to criticism led to appointment of Bradford Morse in June 1991 to head up an independent review of the Narmada Valley Project, the first such review in World Bank history. Bank president Lewis Preston acknowledged that the problems noted in the review were serious, but on June 18, 1992, he announced that "continued Bank support for the Narmada projects is justified" ("Preston Acknowledges Problems in India Narmada Projects," *World Bank News,* June 1992, 8). However, in 1993, the World Bank withdrew support. Unfortunately, the governments of India and of the Indian states involved are continuing to build these dams, while acting with increasing violence against the villagers who resist ("Narmada Update: Violence Escalates," *Friends of the Earth,* Mar.-Apr. 1994, 5). I learned of the World Bank withdrawal too late to rewrite the text. The main point in the text about the contrast of two types of development holds, and the superiority of "another development" becomes still clearer when even the World Bank acknowledges the destructiveness of the dominant current course.

4. Ekins, *A New World Order,* 89. His reference is to "India— Sardar Sarovar (Narmada) Projects: Background Notes," mimeo, World Bank, Washington, D.C.

5. Ibid., 98. Ekins's reference is to Baba Amte, *Cry, the Beloved Narmada* (Anandwan, Chandrapar, India: Maharogi Sewa Samiti, 1989).

6. Rusi Engineer, "The Sardar Sarovar Controversy: Are the Critics Right?" a special report in *Business India*, 30 Oct.-12 Nov. 1989, 99. Quotes are from Ekins, *New World Order*, 99.

5. AGAINST FREE TRADE

1. Denis Goulet, *Mexico: Development Strategies for the Future* (Notre Dame, Ind.: Notre Dame University Press, 1983), 70–71.

2. Tim Padgett, "The Gloom Behind the Boom," *Newsweek*, 28 March 1992, 48.

3. See chapter 3, note 1. The group that initiated this project also included Sandy Dawson, Dean Freudenberger, Christopher Ives, Carol Johnston, and Tokiyuki Nobuhara.

4. Letter by Eve Kummel, *Times* international advertising sales manager, quoted in *Newsday* news release, 26 July 1993.

5. Ibid.

6. THE NEW WORLD ORDER

1. Seymour Melman, *Pentagon Capitalism* (New York: McGraw-Hill, 1970), 1.

2. Seymour Melman and Lloyd J. Dumas, "Planning for Economic Conversion," *The Nation*, 16 April 1992, 526.

3. Betty G. Lall and Joan Tepper Marlin, *Building a Peace Economy* (Boulder, Col.: Westview Press, 1992), 75.

4. "World at War—1992: Fewer Wars—No Danger to the United States," *The Defense Monitor* 21, no. 6 (1992), 2.

5. Daly and Cobb, *For the Common Good*, chap. 2.

Select Bibliography

Cobb, John B., Jr. "Against Free Trade." *Theology and Public Policy* 4, no. 2 (fall 1992): 4–16.

Daly, Herman, and John B. Cobb, Jr. *For the Common Good.* Boston: Beacon Press, 1989.

Ekins, Paul. *A New World Order: Grassroots Movements for Social Change.* London: Routledge, 1992.

Fisher, Julie. *The Road from Rio: Sustainable Development and the Nongovernmental Movement in the Third World.* Westport, Conn.: Praeger Publishers, 1993.

Goulet, Denis. *Mexico: Development Strategies for the Future.* Notre Dame, Ind.: Notre Dame University Press, 1983.

Lall, Betty G., and Joan Tepper Marlin. *Building a Peace Economy.* Boulder, Col.: Westview Press, 1992.

Lea, Stephen E. G., Roger M. Tarpy, and Paul Webley. *The Individual in the Economy: A Survey of Economic Psychology.* New York: Cambridge University Press, 1987.

McFague, Sallie. *The Body of God: An Ecological Theology.* Minneapolis: Fortress, 1993.

Melman, Seymour. *Pentagon Capitalism.* New York: McGraw-Hill, 1970.

Polanyi, Karl. *The Great Transformation.* New York: Octagon Books, 1975.

Rhoads, Steven E. *The Economist's View of the World.* New York: Cambridge University Press, 1985.

Index